LEX ORANDI

LEX ORANDI

OR

PRAYER AND CREED

BY

GEORGE TYRRELL,

AUTHOR OF "HARD SAYINGS," "NOVA ET VETERA" ETC.

> Do men gather grapes of thorns, or figs of thistles? A good tree cannot bring forth evil fruit, neither can an evil tree bring forth good fruit.

New Impression

WIPF & STOCK · Eugene, Oregon

Wipf and Stock Publishers
199 W 8th Ave, Suite 3
Eugene, OR 97401

Lex Orandi
or Prayer and Creed
By Tyrrell, George, SJ
ISBN 13: 978-1-60608-388-8
Publication date 02/03/2009
Previously published by Longmans, Green and Co., 1907

Nihil Obstat:

    ALEX. CHARNLEY, S.J.

           Censor Deputatus.

Imprimatur:

    ✠ FRANCISUS,

           Episc. Southwarcensis.

Religion's all or nothing; it's no mere smile
O' contentment, sigh of aspiration, sir—
No quality o' the finelier tempered clay
Like its whiteness or its lightness; rather, stuff
O' the very stuff; life of life, and self of self.
I tell you, men wont notice. When they do,
They'll understand.

Robert Browning.

similarly any new description of religion will help us to find it whether in ourselves or outside ourselves; or if we have found it, will assure us in our possession of it.

The theological apologist aims at reconciling theology proper (that is, the logically connected statement and analysis of revealed truth) with the rest of our knowledge, through the middle-term of an infallible revelation. When he has established this latter fact by reason, and when the dogmatic theologian has built up his system on the foundation thus given him, we are presented with the purely intellectual aspect of religion as claiming a mental assent proportioned to the force of the general argument.

Such an assent however is infinitely weaker and lower than the assent of faith. But the apologist can go a step further and show also by reason that the assent of faith is a duty—a *rationabile obsequium*. Further than this mere reasoning cannot go.

Allow this scientific and objectively valid proof of religion to be as perfect a demonstration as such matters admit of; yet when presented to this man or that, it will either be rejected altogether or else lie heavily on his mind as an undigested difficulty, until the truth be voluntarily appropriated by him through an act of faith. For the truths of religion like those of history and physical science are directed to life as their end. We accept even these latter only because they explain and fit in with the life that we live, and offer means of its expansion; because they enable us to understand and master our physical and social environment and to appropriate its resources. Had they no direct or indirect bearing upon the interests of our temporal life, or were that bearing wholly obscured, or misconceived as adverse, then no demonstration could force them on our acceptance; they would be merely curious riddles waiting solution. And the demonstrated truths of religion are no more than this to a man until he see their bearing upon his life, or upon certain elements of his life, which they promise to foster and develope; until they offer to him the mastery of a spiritual world whose wealth he desires to appropriate. If the life to which they point be to him in every way uncongenial, strange and violent, their hold on his intellect will be purely external; he will be puzzled, not convinced.

It is not enough therefore for the apologist to connect the truths of theology with the truths of history and science; he must go on to connect the life of religion with the rest of our life, and to show that the latter demands the former. This is to some extent the aim of that " affective " apologetic which appeals to the will and affections by enlarging on the beauties and utilities of religion, on the contentment and happiness that accompany a life of faith and love. But this appeal is but a seduction and temptation, a source of bias and prejudice, unless it can be further shown that, under certain conditions and limitations, utility is dependent upon truth ; that if beliefs react fruitfully upon life it is because they have first been shaped by life as instruments for its own advancement; that no belief can be universally and perpetually useful unless it also be true; and finally that, in the case of the Christian creed, the experience of the Christian " orbis terrarum " offers a criterion as to such universal and perpetual usefulness.

The present volume runs more or less upon these lines.

Two silent assumptions underlying its whole contention must here be brought into clear recognition, lest the entire structure prove a castle in the air, compact but baseless.

I.

First, it is assumed that as in the concrete simplicity of man's spiritual nature we may usefully distinguish an æsthetic, a scientific, a moral sense, so also we must distinguish a religious sense whose developments, healthy or unhealthy, furnish an experimental criterion of belief, one whose verdict is often not less considerable than that of a strictly intellectual criterion. In thus making a certain sort of life one of the tests of truth, we assume that such a life is an admitted and easily recognisable fact. There can of course be no more question of a separate religious "faculty" in the old sense, than of a separate moral faculty. Our conscious life viewed on the one side presents the unbroken continuity and rich simplicity of a progressively accumulating apprehension of the world we live in; and on the other, of a progressive adaptation of our total practical and volitional attitude in regard to the world so apprehended. Only for convenience of thought do we break this really unbroken life and movement into various components. When we give man a "moral sense" we mean that his love of what is right in conduct (personal, social or political) is not reducible to his animal self-love, to his instinct of physical self-preservation, but is an independent and higher co-factor of his life. Similarly as to his love of truth or of beauty, *i.e.* his scientific and his æsthetic sense. These all are conceived as distinct apprehensions, loves, and interests of his spiritual nature, not reducible to one another, but harmoniously coordinated in one and the same life or movement.

We may ask (i) : Is there then a "religious sense" reducible to none of these? and if so (ii) What is its place in this coordination?

(i)

Is religion merely, as it is undoubtedly in its more primitive forms, a means to temporal ends, to personal protection and advantage, or to social and national prosperity? In that case no special sense, no special love is required. God is simply viewed as one of the agencies we have to consider in our struggle for physical existence.

Is God simply a necessity of the mind, a *sine qua non* of our philosophical account of the universe? As such He satisfies our love of truth, our scientific sense.

Is religion, as it is according to Aristotle, simply a department of justice or duty? or is it simply subservient to good conduct in providing new motives and sanctions? There are many whose religion is part of their general propriety; who are religious because they are moral, rather than conversely; or who use their religion as a prop for their morals. So far, the moral sense suffices, nor is any special "religious sense" required.

Or, finally, is religion simply an æsthetic necessity; something needed for the refinement and beautifying of life, a golden halo of illusion framing the world of prosaic fact? It is indeed all that, as the Chateaubriands tell us; but is it no more?

One answer suggests that the religious sense is more than the moral or the scientific or the æsthetic sense only because it is their sum-total; it is the sense and desire of the Ideal in all these three departments; it is the disinterested self-sacrificing love and service of the good, the fair and the true. "God" were thus but the personification of this endlessly unfolding and receding Ideal for whose realisation we hunger in the measure that we put off the animal and put on the spiritual. He would be a mere symbol of all the still undeveloped possibilities of goodness latent in the human soul. Our striving and yearning towards Him would be as that of a child towards its own manhood, towards what it hopes to be in some far future. In other words our hunger would be for "the divine," rather than for God,—for "the divine" in our own inward character and aspirations, and in the world around us so far as it could be shaped by our labour.

But even were this essentially endless labour to be accomplished man could never say: "I have found Him whom my soul loveth, I will hold Him and will not let Him go;" for he would hold, not the Creator but the creature; not the Infinite but the finite, albeit illumined, permeated and transfigured by the irradiation of the Infinite.

The experience of life proves the insufficiency of this answer by the slow production within us of two following convictions fatal to its claims.

(a) In the first place the disappointment and dissatisfaction which we feel time after time in the face of our present attainments, as contrasted with that further stage of the Ideal which lies far away on the new horizon within our range of vision, is gradually recognised as an inevitable shadow that deepens as it moves with us pace by pace. We awake to the hitherto neglected truth, unwanted and unwelcome in the hopeful buoyancy and vigour of our first start on the upward journey, that the road has no ending; that there can be no finality in any conceivable attainment of such goodness and truth and beauty as we are searching for; that no measure of the Ideal however vast can equal the Absolute; that the fault lies in the insufficiency, not of our present attainments, but of all conceivable attainments. As the pleasure-seeker may at last make experimental proof of the worthlessness of his ends and turn from the life of sense to the life of the spirit; so to the idealist there often comes a day when the thought of the finitude of even his most spiritual aims creeps over him like a black cloud, a "dark night of the soul" filling him with weariness and *ennui*. "Vanity of vanities" is the verdict of the higher, no less than of the lower, experience of life. Nay, it is those who have aimed highest, who have laboured hardest, who have wrestled most fiercely with error, with evil, with deformity of every sort, who best realise how disappointing their utmost attainments must ever be; how infinitely more, how absolutely different in kind, must be That which would lend life a solid value,—That, in contrast with which the Ideal when weighed in the opposite scale is found altogether wanting. That we are capable of such a judgement and condemnation makes it evident that we possess within us as a standard or criterion, a certain obscure consciousness of the Absolute and Infinite. That we are dissatisfied, not only with what the Ideal gives us, but, by anticipation, with all it could ever possibly give us is proof that there is a higher love-power within us which must seek its object elsewhere.

If the love of God comprehends and unifies, it also endlessly transcends and is uniquely distinct in kind from every sort of personal affection towards our fellow-men and fellow-creatures individually or collectively; from all devotion to, and enthusiasm for the Ideal—for the Good, the Fair and the True; even from the love of God's will and kingdom upon earth. For it is the love of That which is the *prius*, the source, the explanation, the end of such affections; the root of all values, the foundation of all realities, the complement of all imperfections; of That which alone possesses what they singly and collectively lack, and by lacking are unsatisfying apart from It — infinitude, eternity, sovereign independence and reality. As an affection, our love of the Absolute is more than generically distinct from all our other loves; for it is not "one of them," it is not alongside, but over and through and behind them all, implicit from the very first, explicit only at the very last. On its negative side it might be described as a sense of incurable dissatisfaction with anything that is less than infinite and eternal, with the utmost conceivable extension of finite good; a sense that is deepened and enriched just in the measure that we push out experimentally in all directions vainly seeking the Absolute in the plane of the Relative, the equivalent of the Creator in terms of the creature. "I questioned the earth and it answered: 'I am not thy God,' and all that was therein did answer the self-same. I questioned the sea and the abyss and every living thing that crept therein; and they answered: 'We are not thy God; seek higher.' I questioned the breezes that blow; but the wide air and all its denizens replied: 'Anaximenes hath erred: we are not God;' and I questioned the heaven, the sun, moon and stars and they too answered: 'Neither are we that God whom thou seekest.' Then said I to all these things gathered round the gates of my senses: 'Ye have told me that my God is not you; tell me then what He is.' And with one accord they all answered: 'He hath made us.'"[1]

If on its negative side this love is a revolt against the finitude of the finite, the transiency of the transient, the relativity of the relative, however strongly these may draw us and bind us to themselves in virtue of their

[1] Aug. *Conf.* x. 6.

limited goodness; it is, on its positive side, a felt attraction towards That which, like some dark star, is the source of all our perturbation, restlessness and discontent; towards That which is given to our consciousness directly only in this very feeling of inexplicable hunger, but of which inference and reflection give us some faltering knowledge that Faith alone can make real for us so long as we still walk by Faith, and see, not face to face, but through a glass darkly.

(b) But not only does the experience of life convince us that if the religious sense in some way includes, it also goes beyond our conception and desire of the Ideal; that "the divine" is not God, but something to be measured against God, something to lead us to Him partly by semblance yet far more by contrast; it also convinces us that the attempt to make the pursuit of the Ideal our supreme end, our highest life, to the exclusion of any other, leads to disaster, not so grossly, but just as surely, as the attempt to find our end in the life of the body; and for the same reason, namely, that it is an inversion of right order founded on a misconception of our spiritual nature and destiny. Even the divine is not God, and God has made us for Himself and our soul is restless till it rest in Him.

Fallen from the spiritual liberty of sonship into the bondage of sense, into the slough of carnality and worldliness, paralysed and half-dead through that forfeiture of self-control which is the wages of sin, the soul that would be free, that would find its lost self again, cries out: "Wretched man that I am! who shall deliver me?"

And the answer comes, as to an Augustine: "What these have done," women and children and weaklings of all sorts, "why should not I?" I will deliver myself; I will arise, and go, and retrace my steps and unlearn my bad habits one by one, and clothe myself with virtues, and live only for what is divinely fair and good, and so recover my lost liberty.

So presented, this impulse, dictated chiefly by a horror of servitude, a longing for lost freedom and self-possession, seems scarcely religious in any specific sense; yet it may easily take on a semblance of religion. A man may explicitly recognise the Ideal of every sort as the object of God's will and command; he may devote himself thereto disinterestedly; he may be aware of a consequent conformity of his own will to the divine, and yet he may not make that conformity his direct and principal aim—he may give himself to God's work, God's will, God's cause, and yet not give himself to God. Moreover he may understand that if weaklings have lived that ideal life which he vainly desires to live, they have done so by the grace and help of God, and he may have recourse to that aid in the interests of the end he has set before himself. Yet with all this he does not transcend the limits of an ideal life; his governing aim is not the possession of God but the realisation of the divine; religion is his aid, not his end. He is indeed nigh to the Kingdom of God but he is not there yet. He has not yet read his spiritual nature and its needs aright, and is putting what is secondary in the first place; in making religion an instrument of the ideal life, he is doomed to the inevitable failure which is the penalty of every violation of right order and of the eternal will.

Foot-sore and weary after many stumblings and haltings on his homeward journey, he at last sinks by the way disheartened. Not only is he beaten in the effort to realise what he falsely deems his highest life and end, but the very Ideal itself palls upon him with its finitude, its relativity, when considered out of its true connection. It too, no less than the husks of the swine, proves "vanity and vexation of spirit"—a noble illusion, no doubt, a magnificent bubble, but still a bubble, an illusion.

Not till these lessons of experience are well learnt does God run forward to meet the returning soul, and by His kiss and embrace suddenly waken and call forth that wholly other kind of life and strength hitherto latent and buried—the life of personal communion with Himself, the strength of self-conquering love. Herewith the missing keystone is set in the tottering arch; the crookedness of man's former aim is adjusted, and the ideal life, in being duly thrust down to the second place below the life of religion and set in its right context, receives again its lost meaning and worth, and in the strength of divine love its yoke is made easy and its burden light. It is now recognised, not as an endlessly disappointing effort to find God, but as an ever more satisfying effort to utter Him whom we have already found; to express and reproduce in terms of the finite and relative that Absolute and Infinite whose secret presence is given us by the "religious sense;" to adjust ourselves, by movement and action, more perfectly to the focus of its influence; to bring ourselves ever into a truer affective relation with it, finding in this affection the very end and aim of every other spiritual effort.

It is thus that man at last finds and realises himself when he gives up seeking himself, or rather, seeking a false ideal of himself that is nowhere to be found: "In seeking myself, I lost both myself and Thee; in seeking Thee, I found both Thee and myself." Let him once see that his principal end is personal communion with God and fix his attitude accordingly, and forthwith all other ends in becoming duly subordinate become at once intelligible and realisable.

The "religious sense" is therefore something distinct from the moral, the scientific, the æsthetic "sense;" and even from the combination of all three in what we might call the "sense of the Ideal" or of the Divine. It is the "sense of God," of the Absolute and Infinite. And by a "sense" in all these cases we mean the consciousness of certain realities to which we have to adapt our conduct, of certain feelings and intentions with regard to the same.

(ii)

Since then we must analyse the simplicity of our spiritual life into these factors, what place, it may be asked, does the "religious sense" hold in their harmonious coordination?

It is only partly true to say that its

relation to the other spiritual senses, moral, æsthetic, intellectual, is somewhat that of the head to the members of an organism, or of a constitutional monarch to his people. It is partly true because it excludes that "absolutist" conception which would deny all independent rights to the non-religious interests of life as though they too were not indispensable co-factors of man's total perfection ; because it insists that a bodiless head is no less a monstrosity than a headless body and that the religious life has need of the moral, the æsthetic and the intellectual no less than these have need of it. It is perhaps a truer metaphor which relates religion to the rest, as the soul is related to the body. For, the sense of the Absolute is given not *beside*, but *in* and *with* and *through* the sense of the Ideal in every department : it is the sense of That over against which every conceivable Ideal is felt to be infinitely inadequate, since something greater must always be thinkable ; of That which draws us to the centre of a sphere whose surface we must traverse for ever in pursuit of the Ideal; of That which is the source of an incurable spiritual restlessness till we learn to rest in It. It is the sense of that ultra-reality which lies behind all finite reality as an ever invisible Sun whose form and splendour is hid from us by cloud-barriers of varying density, and whose light is known to us only as luminous mist. In the Ideal, in the True, the Good and the Fair, we have the Finite variously transfused and transfigured by the rays of the Infinite, forcing upon us the conception of an illuminating source beyond, whose precise form and nature lies shrouded in mystery.

He who lives disinterestedly and self-sacrificingly for the Ideal, lives so far for the will of God,—for what God wills; but he does not make this coincidence of his own will with the Divine his explicit and principal aim. If through false reasoning he reflexly excludes or ignores the life of divine love and communion, and puts the Ideal explicitly as his supreme end, he is doomed to the failure which attends every perversion of nature.

It is then the function of religion to discern and make explicit that confused sense of the Absolute which is implicit and presupposed in the spontaneous and sincere pursuit of the Ideal; to bring forward and foster that subconscious love of God which is involved in the conscious love of that which God wills; to find in the proved insufficiency of the latter an argument for the absolute necessity of the former.

Such then is that life of religion; such, that sense of God, that love and need of God, which in the following pages are used as a criterion of truth. Deepest in man's spiritual nature the religious sense is often the last to come to full explicitness; yet it is as natural to man as are the perceptions and affections of his moral, intellectual, or æsthetic life. If the life of religion is thus natural, beliefs that universally and perpetually foster this life must be true to the ultimate nature of things.

II.

The other silent assumption underlying much that follows is one which at first sight might seem in conflict with that technical theology which defines the Grace of Christ as being beyond not only the executive powers, but also the very exigencies of man's spiritual nature. Prior to more recent controversies on Grace its definition made no explicit reference to such exigencies. St. Thomas Aquinas,[1] following the tradition of his past, finds in man a natural exigency of the face to face Vision of God (*i.e.* of the order of Grace) which however it is wholly beyond man's natural powers to attain since it involves a free self-giving on the part of God. The explanation is that he considers man's nature not philosophically, but historically, as it was and is *de facto* constituted with reference to the supernatural order, not as in the abstract it might have been; that the conception of the hypothetical

[1] *Summa Th.* Pt. I. q. xii. a. 1.

"order of pure nature" had not yet become explicit for theological thought. In every hypothesis, God is as natural to man as the air he breathes. The soul is as plainly constructed for God as a harp is for the hand of the harper; the music of its life is more truly from Him than from itself, though each be full cause in its own kind. When we argue from the exigencies of man's spiritual nature we consider that nature as living and breathing the breath of God's nostrils, not as it were a lifeless corpse. We argue from its action and vital movement, not from its bare structure. This latter is the same, whether for the order of Grace or for the hypothetical order of pure nature. The difference which characterises the supernatural is to be sought in the soul's action, and is to be ascribed to a difference in God's end, intention and operation in regard to man's destiny; in the manner of his indwelling and co-efficiency; in his handling and use of an instrument whose structure admits of, but was not necessarily designed for, application to so high a purpose. Taking God's action and the soul's as two co-efficients of one and the same spiritual life, it is to the character and manner of the former that the difference of its resulting life, as "supernatural" rather than "natural" is due. Considered historically, whether as created in Grace, or as fallen from Grace, or as restored to Grace, man's soul has uniformly breathed the air of a supernatural atmosphere; God's salutary workings in his heart have always been directed, however remotely, to the life of Grace and Glory; of the "order of mere nature" and its exigencies we have no experimental, but only an uncertain deductive knowledge, chiefly negative.

From all this it follows that the spiritual life of man, as it has been *de facto* uniformly from the beginning, and as alone it is known to us experimentally, is exigent of Grace and Glory; is exigent not merely of religion, but of "supernatural" religion, of Christianity. It cannot thrive or flourish in any other atmosphere. To say that from an examination of those exigencies we can deduce all the truths and mysteries of Christianity would be an extravagance; but it is not too much to say, with Pascal, that a study of the human soul as revealed in history offers a riddle to which Christianity alone supplies an answer; that when the confused implications of human action are unfolded and made clear to us in the development of human life, individual and social, the soul is discovered to be *naturaliter Christiana.*

Thus we have a right to say that Christianity is "natural" to man as he has actually been constituted in and for the order of grace; we have a right to bid men look into their own souls and find there a vacancy that Christ only can fill; to show them that His religion is not something heterogeneous to their nature, violently thrust upon them from outside by force of logic or of juridical coercion, but that it is the only true development of a life that is already within them, nay, of their very selves.

This Augustinian standpoint is presupposed in the following pages so far as they furnish an argument not merely for theistic but for specifically Christian beliefs. In the present order Christianity viewed subjectively is the only "natural" religion; it is not Theism *plus* certain other beliefs. Theism is but embryonic Christianity; and Christianity is but developed Theism; "purely natural" religion is mere hypothesis—it is what might have been, but what never was.

Viewed from the standpoint taken in these pages, tested by the criterion of life, of spiritual fruitfulness, the truths of this Christianity cannot be expected to present the same precision and clearness of outline as when deduced from defined premisses and built up into a coherent intellectual system. We can but see men as trees walking; blurred contours; mountain-shapes looming through mist. Yet the verification is not valueless; it is not nothing if approaching the truth from this side, and by this less frequented path, we find what we had a right to expect; it is not nothing if that vague "Power that makes for righteousness" in the souls of men is seen, as we strain through darkness, to shape itself ever more and more into conformity with the familiar beliefs of the Christian tradition.

. . . .

I would fain acknowledge my indebtedness to the writings of others, to those from whose treasures I have, with permission, borrowed extensively and without such quotation marks as honesty had else demanded. But it is better to be satisfied with a disclaimer of all pretence to being more than a weaver of materials gathered from many quarters which in the present fabric may acquire a very different significance from that which was theirs in the original texture from which they have been torn.

G. TYRRELL.

30 July, 1903.

NOTE.—For the leading ideas of this Introduction I am indebted to an essay, since published in the *Dublin Review*, entitled, "Experience and Transcendence," by Baron Friedrich von Hügel, to whom, I may say without exaggeration, I owe more than to all my other teachers put together.

CONTENTS.

	PAGE
INTRODUCTION	v
I. The Sacramental Principle	1
II. The Two Worlds	6
III. The Life of Religion	11
IV. The Life of Prayer	19
V. The Church and the Means of Grace	27
VI. The Two Tables	36
VII. Love and Belief	46
VIII. The Truth of Beliefs	53
IX. Lex Orandi	59
X. The Dark Glass of Mystery	65
XI. Belief in God	71
XII. Belief in Free-will	84
XIII. Belief in Immortality	91
XIV. Belief in the Blessed Trinity	100
XV. Belief in God's Fatherhood	106
XVI. Belief in God's Omnipotence	114
XVII. Belief in God's Goodness and Wisdom (1)	123
XVIII. Belief in God's Goodness and Wisdom (2)	131
XIX. Belief in God as Creator	139

		PAGE
XX. Belief in the Incarnation (1)	.	147
XXI. Belief in the Incarnation (2)	.	154
XXII. Belief in Facts of Religious History	.	164
XXIII. The Prayer-value of other Beliefs (1)	.	172
XXIV. The Prayer-value of other Beliefs (2)	.	180
XXV. The Prayer-value of other Beliefs (3)	.	187
XXVI. Ethical Beliefs	.	194
XXVII. Morality and Religion	.	199
Conclusion	.	205

LEX ORANDI.

I.

THE SACRAMENTAL PRINCIPLE.

EVERY rite and sacrament of the Church has its outward and its inward side; its value in the world of sense and its value in the world of spirit. Of the latter our Saviour says: "It **is** the spirit that quickeneth; the flesh profiteth nothing," and those unacquainted with the idiom of His language, have often supposed that in rebuking one exaggeration He here countenances another; that in insisting on the supreme importance of the spirit, He denies all importance to the flesh. And yet the very metaphor employed—spirit and flesh; soul and body—suggests the true sense of His utterance: namely, that the relation of inward and outward in religion is akin to that of soul and body. Without the spirit, the flesh profiteth nothing; yes, but without the flesh the spirit is inoperative, silent, incommunicable. If God is to enter into practical relations with man, He must in some way become man; He must present Himself to us humanwise; the Idea must become imaginable; the Truth, incorporate; the Word must be made flesh and dwell in our midst. As sacramental in principle, the religion of the Incarnation is consonant with the unchanging exigencies of human nature; it is the ideal religion of humanity.

Ritual, like gesture or intonation, is after all only an extension or supplement of verbal language. Words are a rough algebra of our understanding; that is, of one department of our inner life. If they express feelings, emotions, desires, it is only so far as we have thought about these feelings, symbolised them, classified and named them. Words, actions, conduct, and the like, all taken together constitute the outward expression and embodiment of our hidden spiritual activity. Through them we are made known to one another and learn from one another. The letter, no less than the flesh, is opposed to the spirit in Sacred Writ; as "the flesh

profiteth nothing" so "the letter slayeth."
Again, the meaning is that, apart from the
spirit the letter slayeth, though it is only
through the instrumentality of the letter that
the spirit can impart life to the flesh-clad
spirit of man. The words in which religious
truth is clothed are therefore sacramental;
they belong to the world of sense and also to
the world of spirit; to the apparent, the
relative, the transitory; and also to the real,
the absolute, the eternal.

As we are constituted, the "real" too
often means for us the visible, the palpable,
the tangible; that which strikes on our
outward senses; the letter which slayeth;
the flesh which profiteth nothing. Spirit
seems to us something shadowy, abstract,
unsubstantial. This surface estimate of
things must be inverted; and our whole
upward progress from animalism and
savagery towards rational and spiritual life
consists in slowly effecting this inversion; in
controlling our life and action ever less by
impulse, ever more by idea; in shaping our
conduct to an ever wider apprehension of
things; in guiding ourselves less in the
light of what is present to us here and now,

and more in view of what is distant and future, and finally, of what is infinite and eternal. In other words, our progress lies in practically realising with St. Paul[1] that the things which are seen are temporal, fugitive and unreal; whereas the things which are not seen are eternal, permanent and real in the deepest sense of reality; it is a progress in that Faith·which is the making substantial and evident to ourselves of things hoped-for but yet unseen.

When we speak, then, of religious truths as sacramental, as having a literal and a spiritual value, we should do ill to call the former the *real*, the latter the *figurative* sense, if we meant that what they signified in the natural order were more, and not immeasurably less, "real" than what they signified in the spiritual order. The law of divine grace and mercy figured by the parables of the Prodigal Son and of the Good Samaritan is not less, but far more "real" than the law of gravitation.

The truths of the Creed are not parables, for a parable is, in its literal sense, a deliberate fiction; it does not claim any

[1] 2 Cor. iv. 18.

value as history or science or philosophy; its sole truth is its correspondence to eternal realities—a correspondence of a very inexact and one-sided kind. But the articles of Faith for the most part claim a double truth; a correspondence both to the lower and to the higher order of reality. Thus the Ascension of Christ into Heaven may be viewed both as a fact of history, and as a symbol of His spiritual exaltation. The Eucharistic Presence in like manner: or the Virgin Birth: or the Crucifixion. All are compounded of body and soul; flesh and spirit—the spirit alone quickening, the flesh availing nothing save as the instrument of the spirit.

We propose in a series of short chapters to consider some of the principal truths of our Faith under these two aspects. But first it will be necessary to make ourselves clearer as to the two worlds, the two kinds of reality, with which we have to do; to say more exactly what we mean by the life of Religion, the life of prayer, in order to understand the part which our beliefs play in that life.

II.

THE TWO WORLDS.

ALL our conscious life and movement is swayed by our will—our likes and dislikes; our wants and aversions; by our affection for ourselves or for others; for things, or for persons. First, not in fact, but in order of dependence, come the necessities of our separate and individual life. To exist at all is pre-requisite to any higher sort of life. Our temporal or bodily life depends on our power over that physical world around us with which we are in ceaseless conflict, which claims back every particle of dust that we have wrested from it and built up into our animal organism. Sooner or later our enemy will be victorious: "earth to earth, ashes to ashes, dust to dust"—that is our doom; but to delay that victory as long as possible is the chief aim of our struggle for physical existence. Our success depends largely on the extent to which we understand the machinery of the physical world and can work it in our own interest. Hence the struggle to live and enjoy involves a struggle to know. We feel about tentatively, we taste this and that; try one method and then another; we remember our experiences, classify them, put them together into a system; we frame a theory of the world, its nature and history. And the truer the theory is, the better does it serve as an instrument, a guide, a chart whereby to direct our action fruitfully and to control Nature to our service.

Our very self-interest, however, forces us to cling together, to co-operate, to give to others that we may gain from them. But this herding together occasions the manifestation of a higher and better sort of life, the life of social affection and self-forgetfulness. It reveals to us a new joy and happiness—that of friendship or will-union with others—which thereupon becomes the principal goal of our endeavour. This new life implies a new world, a new system of facts and laws with which we have to set ourselves in correspondence. Here again, in order to learn we must first experiment, and from our experience build up some rude conception of the world of wills—the social world—its nature and its laws.

Compared with this invisible spiritual world, that of physical Nature is mere shadow. For nothing can be more real to me than myself. Self is the very test and measure of all reality. If I ascribe reality to things in Nature, it is only because to understand or deal with them at all I must assume that they are like me in some way, that they are to some degree separate, individual, active, if not actually sentient and conscious, as I am. Children and savages personify everything in Nature. It is only experience and reflection that make us modify this instinctive assumption in various degrees, and teach us how the reality of these things falls short of our own. Furthermore, it is in willing, acting, and originating that we recognise our selfhood or reality. Our dreams or dreamy states, in which we are to a great extent passive, are marked by a sense of unreality; we are not ourselves; we are not all there. We are most real only when we are most free, conscious and energetic.

What does all this imply except that the spirit which acts and wills is alone felt to be "real" in the full sense; and that the world given to our outward senses is shadowy and dreamy, except so far as we ascribe to it some of the characteristics of will and spirit?

Thus the life of friendship and social affection relates us to a system of spiritual realities like ourselves; whereas the solitary and selfish life relates us to a world of appearances and shadows, whose semblance of reality is but a broken reflex of our own.

What, after all, and apart from religion, do we feel to be the most solid and undeniable value that this wretched world can offer us; that without which neither health nor wealth nor fame nor strenuous work can save us from terrible moments of disillusionment and life-weariness; that with which we can bear the loss of all these as not even touching the substance of our heart's treasure; what, but the life of affection and friendship? When to our dying eyes and listless ears all these shall be as idle dreams, yet the failing energies which we shall then, perhaps, summon to return the clasp of some loving hand locked in ours will testify to our conviction that all has not been vanity and vexation of spirit ; that the life of love binds us to reality for ever.

Now religion is the life of friendship with God and with His friends ; it relates us to the most real of all realities—the Divine Will—that which lends all their reality to our created wills, and apart from which they are not even intelligible.

We see then, that in virtue of our twofold nature we live in two worlds—one bodily, the other spiritual ; one the shadow and the sacrament ; the other, the substance and the signified reality.

III.

THE LIFE OF RELIGION.

It is therefore the spirit-world, the will-world, that is real to us beyond every other. In it our soul lives its inmost life, and finds its deepest rest or unrest according as it succeeds or fails in adjusting itself to its laws.

It is in willing and acting that our reality is revealed to us; and we account other things real in so far as they seem to oppose a will to ours. We *are*, each of us, a single "willing," which, however we may analyse it into a sum-total of past and present "willings" from which it results, is, nevertheless, one simple act by which we adapt ourselves to the total situation in which we now find ourselves—the past, behind us; the present, around us; the future, before us. Every instant of our life this "willing" modifies itself and dissolves into something different, in response to a similar transformation of our surroundings. Through that world to which our body belongs, and of which our senses, memory, and understanding take account, we are made aware of other wills which express themselves therein, as we ourselves do, by the sensibly evident results of their action. It is in our *felt* relation to these other wills that our spiritual life and reality consists. That relation is, with regard to each several will, one of agreement and attraction, or of revolt and dislike, or rather of a complex blending of likes and dislikes, according to the innumerable elements into which each moral personality, each total will-attitude, may be virtually resolved. Like the motes in a sunbeam the whole world of wills is in ceaseless commotion; each changing its attitude with regard to all the rest, as moment by moment the shifting situation demands a new response. Wherever we find another will accordant with our own in any particular, we experience a sense of re-enforcement and expansion of our spiritual life and being; and this, in proportion to the nature and extent of the agreement, and the nature and number of wills in agreement. On the other hand, there is a sense of spiritual impoverishment and contraction wherever we recognise a will-force in opposition to our own—a sense as though we were losing hold of that community of souls whose being we share, and were dropping away into the void and nothingness of solitude. By their will-attitude in regard to certain personalities, certain deeds, certain aims, in a word, in regard to certain governing will-attitudes, men can be spiritually classified and brought into that system of relations which constitutes the will-world. A Christian, a republican, a Gladstonian, and such names by which men are grouped together, imply always a common end towards which their wills are set in agreement.

But if any sort of will-union with another is desirable in the abstract (*i.e.*, considered alone and apart from the infinity of other will-relations) yet in the concrete it always involves a relation of disagreement with contrary will-attitudes, and a mingling of pain with pleasure. "No man can serve two masters"; if he love the one, he must hate the other. Hence, while this chaos and contrariety prevails, and pending that process of sifting and settling-down through which the stars of this spiritual firmament tend, perhaps eternally, towards the equilibrium of some system of established constellations, we cannot take mere will-union as an end in itself, or as a decisive motive of action. We may not seek rest in agreement, without asking "Rest in what?" "Agreement with what?" Throughout the whole universe of will-attitudes the difference of evil and good, false and true, fair and foul, passes like a two-edged sword. "Right" is a rule of choice clearly higher than the blind and impotent rule of love which would pull us in every direction at once, and lead us in none. Even if we *might* follow the impulse to be at one with all men, we could not. We may err and falter in our judgment as to what is true, fair, or right; we may turn away from our duty when we know it; but we can never falter in our conviction as to the absolute and imperative character of these will-attitudes; we can never doubt that we *ought* to be in sympathy with men of good-will and out of sympathy with the insincere, the selfish, the low-minded. Now this imperative character of the Absolute is simply the force of that supreme, eternal, eventually irresistible Will, which we call God—that Will to which the whole will-world must be subordinate, and in union or agreement with which each created will is saved and realised, even were it at variance with all the rest. This love of God, this dynamic union with the infinite will, is the very substance and reality of our spiritual living and being; other lovings and agreeings belong to the perfection, but not to the essence of our blessedness.

The true orientation of our will must, therefore, be towards that Supreme Will so far as it is manifested in the will-attitudes of those who live by it—of Christ and of all Christ-like men. We know nothing of that Will in its attitude towards extra-human affairs; we only feel it mingling and conflicting with our own in each concrete action that is submitted to our freedom of choice.

Love is, after all, the very substance of our spiritual life, the bond that binds personalities together, and is to the will-world what gravitation is to the physical. But above all wills there is the will of God; and above all loves there is the love of God; and in this, the life of religion consists. It is exercised in the same acts by which we conquer the chaos of our inward life, and transform it to the pattern of those absolute ideals which are the ends and aims of the Divine will.

Our religious character is something that *results from* this action of our will by which we overcome the chaos that is given us, as it were, a wilderness to till and cultivate. From the fact that our will takes this or that attitude in regard to matters of thought, or conduct, or feeling, it is brought into a relation of harmony or discord with every other will, and takes a new position in the will-world. This sense of our ever-changing relation to other wills, of loving and being loved, of hating and being hated, is, as has been seen, the very reality and substance of our spiritual life, it is the motive and the end of all that labour of transformation in which our will expresses itself. Our own mental, moral, and æsthetic formation, our external and social labour only furnishes a medium, an occasion whereby our relation of agreement or disagreement with other wills may be determined—much as their attitude towards the same performance might determine the relation of sympathy between two artists. St. Augustine notes how strangers in a theatre are for the moment drawn together when they see one another applauding the same thing. The pleasure of this sympathy is of quite another order to the artistic pleasure which is its occasion. The latter is from the agreement of the object with our artistic ideals; the former, from the sense of our solidarity with others. In like manner we cannot do what God wills without in that very act bringing our will closer to His; the ethical act entails the religious result, and if done in view of that result, puts on a religious character.

But, to will the same as another whom we do not know, or whose will we do not know, does not put us into that will-relationship with him in which love consists. It is only when the agreement is revealed that there is that rushing of soul to soul, that sense of reinforcement and enlargement, which is so utterly distinct from the ethical or artistic satisfaction which may be the occasion of the agreement. To know that God wills what we will, gives birth to that expression of will-union, that sense of friendship, which no merely ethical satisfaction in duty done can possibly yield.

Since every action we do is built into our spiritual substance as an eternal possession, and does not pass away like its temporal results in the outer world, it is plain that our union with God, our growth in grace and love, admits of an endless accumulative progress; that we can go on for ever determining our relation to Him (and our relation to others viewed as related to Him) more and more exactly as long as life lasts.

IV.

THE LIFE OF PRAYER.

OBVIOUSLY then it is by conduct, but primarily, by prayer in its widest sense, that this union with the Divine Will is fostered and the soul established and strengthened by the sense of its solidarity with the entire will-world as systematised through Him, who is its indwelling source and end. Union with any part of it that is separated from Him must in the end lead to an absolute solitude of the soul, unloved and unloving, shut apart into that outer darkness which is spiritual death.

Prayer, as here taken, is not merely directed to conduct, but is itself directly effective of that will-sympathy with God which is the richest fruit, as it is also the highest motive, of conduct. The religious effort is directed explicitly to the adjustment of our will to God's: and this, not merely as to ourselves, but as to all things that come under His will, so that in all we shall seek to know and feel and act with Him. Here it is that prayer supplements the narrowness of our practical life and gives us as it were artificial occasions of will-union.

A great part of our spiritual discipline is indeed directed to the "religionising" of our general conduct by its explicit conformity and reference to the Divine Will. We prepare ourselves to do what has to be done, as perfectly as possible, not merely in the ethical interest, for the sake of the work done; not merely that our mind, our impulses, our tastes, our whole personality may be conformed to the absolute impersonal standards of the True, the Good, and the Fair; but in the religious interest; in order that in thus effecting *what* God wills, our will may come closer to His, that His will may be more fully in ours; in fact, that we may dwell in Him and He in us—for in no other way are persons united. Again, as every skill is acquired through self-criticism; so too, some kind of self-examination enters into the practice of religion; we need to stand aside and compare our attainments with our ideals more deliberately than is possible in the haste and pressure of action.

But plainly such spiritual exercises as these, are but the pauses for foresight and retrospection which mingle with every sort of production; differing only in this, that they are directed to the adjustment and criticism of the religious aspect of our life. They are directed to living religiously; they impart a religious quality or tinge to our moral life, but they are not strictly exercises of the life of religion. A man at his daily work is living for his family, but he returns from his labour to the enjoyment of family life. Our whole life must be *for* God, but only part of it can be *with* God. This latter involves a certain contemplative and mystical effort whereby we consciously bring ourselves and are brought into an affectionate sympathy with the Divine Will viewed personally; it means a continual growth in the love, not only of those things which God loves, but, through and in them, of the Divine Lover. For however closely connected, the two things are not only distinct, but even separable, and sometimes separated. One can rest in the work without passing on to its author; men can love justice, truth, and goodness, can feel the absolute and imperative character of their claims, and yet fail to recognise them as the expression of a personal will; they can love God's laws, but not the law-giver. But the love of an abstract law is not the sort of love that binds us to the will-world and gives us our spiritual subsistence.

The love that binds us to other wills is not to be conceived statically, as a hard and fast iron band; it is a process of continual adjustment, which may at times seem to be stilled only because the two wills move parallel and at the same rate. But since no living will is ever at rest, but transforms itself ceaselessly into something new, love or the union of wills is essentially a "becoming." Relatively to us, to whom it is gradually disclosed in the measure that we correspond to it, the Divine Will is ever transforming and developing itself; and our union with it involves a like self-transforming on our part.

The mystical life consists in this process. It interfuses itself spontaneously in various degrees of frequency, continuity, and intensity, with the rest of our life, according to the measure of our graces and of our fidelity to better things, *i.e.*, dependently on the free exercise of the Divine Will and of our own, whose times and seasons need not necessarily coincide. "Spiritual exercises" in the proper sense—those that are not merely directed to the "religionising" of our conduct — are directed to this work of harmonising our wills with God's, *i.e.*, to the increase of personal love, or as is commonly said, to converse with God. Instead of waiting till we are moved, we seek to move ourselves; and by memory, reflection, consideration, and inquiry, we multiply the chances of our hearts being kindled by some new aspect of the Divine Goodness.

No otherwise are our human affections deepened. A certain leisureliness is the condition of any very firm and lasting bond between soul and soul. Nowhere are family ties of affection stronger than where the lives are somewhat narrow and vacant of conflicting interests, which, like thorns, spring up and choke the seed of love. The rush and multifariousness of a busy life are incompatible with the brooding habit by which love is fostered and matured. The treasuring and pondering of words spoken, of deeds done, of looks and smiles that open vistas into the inward self, fan the flame of affection as surely as spiritual absence and forgetfulness tend to extinguish it. The moral and spiritual significance of our so-called "idle" musings cannot be too highly estimated; especially when we acknowledge that our deepest life and reality is that of our affection, our will-action, whereof our outer action is but the contingent and ever imperfect expression. When our hands are still and our voice silent, our will pursues its ceaseless evolutions from form to form, and seeks new adjustments of its position relatively to all other wills. As the stream of our imaginings, memories, and reflections, flows past, our will is now drawn, now thrust away, never still for an instant. Hence the educative value of every sort of contemplation, artistic or religious. It is with the latter we are here concerned—that by which we muse upon God as revealed to us inwardly and outwardly.

This is the essence and end of the contemplative effort, and surely it is simple enough, looked at from this point of view. If, to some extent (to be defined later), the character of the Divine Will is revealed in the world of necessity, if the wisdom and power of God are written in the book of physical Nature for those who have eyes to see, yet it is only because their results resemble those of our own wisdom and power, and because we ascribe them to an agency like ourselves that they tell us anything of God at all. It is through self, through man, through the world of freedom and will, that we get to know God as a personality, as a possible object of personal love and affection. It is in the relative and unsatisfying goodness of the human will, that the absolute and satisfying goodness of the Divine Will is revealed to us; even as the light of the hidden sun might be revealed to us in the reflected brilliancy of the moon or the planets. He is the Will, from conformity to which every human character derives all its true lovableness, whether inborn or self-wrought. It is in men that He, the hidden God, is to be sought, studied, and loved—not in abstractions like Truth and Righteousness, but in concrete actions and will-attitudes, in "whatsoever things are true, honest, just, pure, lovely, and of good report." This is the proper field of contemplative search. We are not moved to love by the colourless universals and thought-frames, into which these living realities are forced for scientific purposes — by such divine attributes as Wisdom, Justice, Truth, and the like. What moves us is this or that concrete deed of goodness, which reveals the present attitude of the living wills, divine and human, that gave birth to it—this unique and never-to-be-repeated act of mercy, or of courage, or of self-sacrifice, or of truth and fidelity, in which a flash of God's infinite glory lightens on us through some momentary rift in the veil of the finite. These are real facts and events in the will-world in regard to which we have to determine our own attitude so as to come into relation with God, whose will is revealed and uttered in every good will. Hence, every act of right love that binds us to other wills by sympathy and conformity, binds us with a new bond to the Divine Will as soon as this is recognised as a personality, as the source of all goodness, as the centre and unitive principle of the will-world—indwelling, all-pervading, all-transcending.

V

THE CHURCH AND THE MEANS OF GRACE.

Since the attitude of the Supreme Will is not known to us directly, but only through its manifestations in every sort of human goodness, it is by attuning ourselves to this world of finite goodness that we come into harmonious unity with God. Only through contact and union with that which is already magnetised are we brought under the mysterious magnetising influence of the Divine and ourselves magnetised; only, that is, through contact and union with the Mystical Christ, with the sanctified humanity centred round Jesus, in and with which the Divine Will offers itself to our love. As we perfect our taste or our judgment by the study of master-minds, so in the matter of religion we turn to the great masters, to Saints and Prophets, to study their attitude

Godwards, to be affected by it and to throw ourselves into it. As in every other respect, so in this, our life depends on society for its education and development. The deeds and words of holy God-loving men and women, are the food of our souls; it is there that their will-attitude is revealed to us.

In its actual and historical form this communion of saints, this society of God-loving men is called the Invisible Church, and finds its head and unitive principle in Christ, the simple fulness of whose perfection is analysed and broken up for our study and help in the various measures of Christliness shared by other men, in whom its inexhaustible potentiality is brought to ever greater explicitness by its application to an infinite variety of circumstances and conditions. It is to this society, to this many-membered corporate Christ of all times and ages, that we must go to school in order to perfect ourselves in the art of Divine love and to bring our will into more extensive and delicate sympathy with God's.

For "no man hath seen God at any time" nakedly and face to face; and vain is the effort of that false neo-platonic mysticism that would seek Him by intellectual abstraction in the very emptiest of our class-notions, rather than in the living fulness of His spiritual creations. Only as mirrored in the progressively purified human soul is He brought more and more within the grasp of human apprehension. "No man cometh to the Father but by Me" is true in its measure of the mystical and corporate Christ no less than of the personal Christ; for it is in that Christ, in that sanctified humanity clustered round the Cross of Calvary that His goodness is incarnate and revealed to us. Union with God means necessarily and identically union with the whole body of His Saints, with the choicest flower, the richest fruit of humanity; with those who like Christ have gone forth in all ages and peoples as sheep in the midst of wolves, self-sacrificed victims to the cause of God; whose blood mingled with that of Eucharistic chalice wins forgiveness and grace for their destroyers; with those who have sown in tears that others might reap in joy; who have failed a thousand times that others might succeed at last, who have laboured hard and long that others might enter quickly and easily into the fruit of their labours; whose deaths are precious in the sight of God, and, in union with that of the Crucified, are daily accepted by Him as a pure, holy, and spotless sacrifice of praise.

Between us and this Invisible Church, this mystical Christ, the visible Church mediates as a divinely appointed instrument of communication. Every spiritual movement or enthusiasm that unites the hearts of multitudes and fires their love, tends spontaneously and by the law of its nature to fashion some kind of social organism or institution for the furtherance of its own development; and from the first the cause of God's Kingship over souls has ever been furthered by the instrumentality of a visible Church, union with which and submission to which is enjoined solely as a means, a measure, an expression of voluntary union and spiritual sympathy with the Invisible Church—with Christ and with all the best and greatest and most Christ-like souls that have ever lived. It is ultimately and only to their purely spiritual authority, to their compelling goodness that we submit ourselves gladly and freely, when we yield obedience to the lawful rules and ordinances of the hierarchic institution, not grudgingly nor of necessity, but as cheerful givers. As members of the visible Church, we share in those communised fruits of its collective spiritual experience and labour which have been accumulating from age to age; we are born, as it were, not into the bosom of a solitary waste to find out everything for ourselves, but into that of a rich and complex spiritual civilisation whose treasures we have only to appropriate; whose life we share; by whose spirit, whose ideas, enthusiasms, energies, we are, not so much taught as, sympathetically infected and stimulated.

It is then to the civilising and schooling of our souls that the whole apparatus of Christianity, viewed as an external religious institution is directed. As à Kempis[1] points out, there are two tables spread for the soul's nourishment in the Visible Church — the table of the Divine Word and the table of Sacramental Grace; and it is by the use of these that the spirit is exercised in conformity with God's will, *i.e.*, in charity.

Both tables—the Word and the Sacraments—are called "Means of Grace." Before

[1] Bk. iv. c. xi. 4.

enquiring into the difference and correlation of these means or instruments, we must be clearer as to their common effect.

Grace is the Love of God or Charity; that is, a relation of will-agreement and personal affection between ourselves and God; not merely a community of ends and aims, such as might exist between two who had never heard of one another, but a union or identity of wills in which each becomes object to the other; enspheres and embraces the other with the embrace of its affection; a union consequent on, and conducive to, a union of aims; yet not created merely by the fact of two wills loving the same thing, converging towards the same point, but by their loving and absorbing one another in consequence. Under whatever metaphor, spatial or otherwise, we may represent will-union and indwelling, it is neither more nor less than mutual love: even if we throw aside the old philosophy, which viewed the will as a separable limb of the spiritual organism, as a superadded "faculty," and recognise that it is only another name for the free personal *ego*, we shall still find ourselves in harmony with those who say that Grace is simply the indwelling of God, since the union of wills and loves is the union of persons: "I in them, and Thou in Me, that they may be made perfect in one." In this way of putting it, it is also clear how grace is a sort of strength imparted to the soul, and, therefore, is spoken of in the terms of a quality or property; for the love of another is a source of new spiritual strength. Even our narrowest self-love is a strength; and we can do wonderful things through the force of selfishness and self-will; but when we bind another personality to our own, this force seems to be more than doubled, and we can do and suffer for the *alter ego* far more than for our solitary self. Even the most timorous animals grow bold and strong in defence of their young; and the spiritual strength and energy imparted by filial, fraternal, parental, or conjugal love is matter of common observation. What wonder if the love of God and of Christ should steel men even to martyrdom at times! or that a Paul should say: "I can do all things through Christ who strengtheneth me!"

"The law came by Moses, but Grace and Truth came by Jesus Christ." Love is the fulfilling of the Law both as substituting an infallible instinct of the Divine Will for a body of ethical precepts and prohibitions whose guidance must fail us in a thousand matters; and then, as not merely pointing the way, but as giving us the desire and strength to walk in it. Sacraments and means of Grace or Love are characteristic of the Christian dispensation. The bare knowledge of the Ideal—of what is ethically just and right in regard to God and man, does not necessarily bring with it the inspiration and love that is needed for the sacrifices demanded by the law; and in failing to do so it is rather an occasion than a remedy of sin, turning what were previously sins of ignorance into sins against conscience. Yet God cannot give, in the world of freedom and will, what we do not desire to receive; He must prepare the appetite before He can satisfy it. And, in spiritual education, the Law precedes Grace, that man may learn his need of love, and the insufficiency of cold ethical light. The *bona fide* savage, content with, or, rather, unaware of, his moral degradation, does not cry: "O wretched man that I am! Who shall deliver me from the body of this death?" The first step towards his redemption is to create in him a sense of sin, and a hunger for deliverance. He must learn that the most enlightened self-love is not strong enough for the burden of the cross—for pursuit and conquest of the Ideal; and that it is only the love of others, and above all, the love of God in Christ, that can inspire the needful force of will.

However directly advantageous it may be to the separate individual, the ultimate scope of every true law, ethical or civil, is the general advantage of all. In some sort, the love of all is its motive and its end, and until the individual is inspired with that same selfless motive, he can neither rightly apply, nor interpret, nor fulfil the law. Self-love gives neither the right key nor the force to turn it. Thus then "love is the fulfilling of the law," *i.e.*, it gives an instinctive knowledge of what to do, and the power to do it. And this is the commonly observed characteristic of personal love; it needs no law to direct or compel it: *Ama, et fac quod vis.*

VI.

THE TWO TABLES.

All private devotion needs to be regulated and brought into harmony with those public and divinely established standards furnished in the liturgy and rites of the Catholic religion which are the fruit of the collective spiritual experience of past ages. Not that the authority of the Past is to fetter the growth of the Future; or that social uniformity is to crush individual liberty. Eccentricity is not individuality. Not till we have learnt and appropriated from society the best that is known and attained, have we a right to venture a step beyond and include all this in some further attainment of our own. Else our deviation from the normal is one of defect, of ignorance and weakness; we have not overtopped the line, but fallen short of it.

The Psalter, the Prophets, the Old Testa-

ment history, the Gospels, the Epistles—
these are the outcome of the Church's inspiration from the beginning. By these she tries to perfect us stage by stage in that spirit of Christ progressingly revealed in the deeds and utterances set before us in the Sacred Scriptures; to bring our wills into the same Godward attitude as that of the patriarchs, prophets, apostles, martyrs, and saints; and through them, as it were preparatively, into the will-attitude of Christ Himself—the supreme ideal of conformity. As this is the end, so it is the key to the right use of the "ministry of the word."

Besides, however, those elements of the word-ministry that are directed explicitly to the cultivation of divine love, there are others whose scope is that right-ordering of our conduct which is a condition and a result of love, but is not love itself. Such elements are, practical exhortation, ethical and ascetic direction, penitential discipline and the rest; which look, not to the life of religion (of which divine love is the very substance and not a mere quality), but to the "religionising" of life; which subserve the ethical effort rather than the mystical.

From the conception of Grace already set forth it will not be hard to see the manner in which the soul is fed at the table of the Divine Word, namely, through an appeal to the individual intelligence and affection; through the infection of that spirit revealed in the words and deeds and whole religious will-attitude of Christ and His saints, as set before us in the Sacred Scriptures and records of the past, or in the liturgy, preaching and teaching of the Christian Church. In all this, our co-operation is essential, we must eat and digest the bread that is put into our hands, not thrust down our throats; there is need of a contemplative or mystical "endeavour," by which we strive to throw ourselves into the spiritual attitude and affection thus revealed to us; to see and to feel with Christ and His members; to raise ourselves to that level of inspiration which finds utterance in the psalms or prayers or liturgical worship of the Church. These are, as it were, the classical masterpieces, the public standards of spiritual taste and feeling, according to which our spontaneous inspirations should be corrected and educated.

Truly, as à Kempis says, all sacred writing must be read intelligently by the aid of the same spirit which inspired it; we must, so far as possible, throw ourselves into the circumstances, conditions, and dispositions of the writer, in whose words we have not a naked and absolute revelation of the Divine, but one that is clothed in the swaddling-bands of human infirmity. And when through these veils and wrappings the hidden spirit has passed into our own hearts, it must there re-clothe itself in our own words and images and receive the mould of our individuality. The prayer of another can never be wholly our own; at best it is Jacob before his father in the garments of Esau.

Besides our direct intercourse and relation with the Divine Will, there is another way in which we are referred to it through our solidarity with others, as parts of a living organism—of the many-membered mystical Christ. As members of this created will-world we share in that love which the Whole offers to God, and in that with which He in return embraces the Whole. This distinction between corporate and private capacity obtains in human relationships. The tie of consanguinity and the tie of personal dearness may co-exist in the same individual and may each found a separate title to love. As incorporated with the body of Christ we each share in its collective action and attitude towards God, and are enriched by the communised blessings which are poured upon it. When Christ says: "No man cometh to the Father but by Me," we may refer these words both to the invisible and the visible Church. To the former, inasmuch as it is only by association with the Christlike that our will is schooled into conformity with that of Christ, and so brought to the Father; for, in solitude our religious faculty (*i.e.*, our capacity of willunion with God) would lie dormant. But the words may also be referred to the visible Church, of which Christ as Man is the Head and Founder, and which is the effective sacrament and symbol of the spiritual Church. Here, too, none can sincerely desire the corporate graces and privileges who wilfully refuse to belong to the organism, and to be visibly united with the visible Christ through His visible Body. And of this visible union the sacraments are the means.

Through them it is that the Church measures out and distributes the riches of Divine love and favour bestowed upon her corporately. On our part they are, so to say, acts of union or contact with her, which, like our other acts, are, on their timeless and spiritual side, an abiding possession of the soul, and establish, each of them, a tie with her, which endures for ever as an element of our personality. By each of them we are rooted more deeply in that sacred soil, and draw a richer nutriment from it.

Chief of them all is the Lord's Supper, which is *par excellence* the sacrament of communion or identification with Christ and His brethren in which the relation established by baptism is developed, deepened, and confirmed. As a sacrifice it is the great act of love or will-union that passes between God and His Church : a renewal of those acts by which, in the person of her Head and of all her martyrs, confessors and saints, the Church has loved and obeyed even unto death and in return has been exalted and received a name above every name. As a sacrament it makes us, in virtue of our incorporation, sharers in that sacrifice and its fruits—in the love given and the love received. Of its very nature, as an experience of our corporate, not of our separate, life, sacramental love and will-union is less sensible and definite, albeit more fundamentally characterising, than personal love. What the civil state or community to which we belong does or suffers, does not tell on us so directly, nor is it felt so consciously as what we do or suffer personally, but eventually it is of more vital and far-reaching consequence.

Supernatural grace or love is that power which comes from will-union with God—the Infinite and Eternal Will ; which is, therefore, an unlimited all-embracing love in sympathy with the Divine. Every love is an association by which the will-strength of the associated units is augmented ; each can do and suffer more for the sake of the rest than he could even do or suffer for his own sake solely. It is, therefore, by association, and in society, that we get power to fulfil the law so far as it makes for the good of that society, and of those whose fate love has linked with our own. And this is what makes association with the Christian Society a means of grace and a condition of an eternal life not otherwise realisable. This is the special grace that flows to us from those sacramental acts through which we multiply the bands and ligaments which tie us as grafts to the mystical vine. This is the *gratia Christi* by which we are associated with Christ and His members, and find in the love of them the strength to fulfil the law of love, as He did. It is to this super-added strength that St. Paul ascribes the abundance of his own labour and sufferings: "Yet not I, but the grace of God in me"; or again: "I live, yet not I" (*i.e.*, not the separate I), "but Christ liveth in me."

The ideal "Prayer-Exercise" is, therefore, to be found in the Eucharistic office, in the combination of the ministry of the Word, with the ministry of the Sacraments. First, the soul is prepared individually by confession and prayer and psalmody and praise; by instruction and exhortation; above all, by the holy Gospel, and thus brought into harmony with the soul and will of the mystical Christ. Then, in the sacred mysteries, as making one thing with Christ and the whole Church, it takes part in the great interchange of love between God and redeemed humanity; which is also the assertion and confirmation of the solidarity that makes us members one of another. The Eucharist is the expression and embodiment of that spiritual act of charity, by which God, and the Church united with Christ, are bound together with a new bond : " I in them and thou in Me, that they may be made perfect in one."

We may surely look back with something like envy on the days when this public Prayer-Exercise was more easily followed by the crowd than is possible now that its language—originally the rude dialect of the people—has died out of popular use. There are many advantages in the present practice but they are necessarily purchased at the sacrifice of other advantages. While we affirm the former we must not overlook the latter, though we may not as yet see a means of combining them both.

The archaic language, music, and ritual has by mere lapse of time acquired a value, originally lacking to it, which now appeals to the historic and æsthetic sense of the cultured few; but what of the uncultured many? On the other hand familiar simplicity often leads through vulgarity to profanity; and a return to primitive practice might be a return to primitive disorder, to the Babel of the Corinthian agape.

VII.

LOVE AND BELIEF.

As a school of dogmatic teaching in faith and morals the Christian Church gives us, as has been implied, the highest mental expression of the will-world that the collective understanding of believers has elaborated by the spiritual labour of centuries—the joint work of the old-world prophets, completed by Christ and developed by the Church. Therein she gives us an external and authoritative standard by which our personal religious understanding is to be rectified. The right aim and justification of such social and public standards is not to cramp and restrain, but to stimulate and provoke private initiative. If the Church's teaching hampers us, it is because we misuse it or misconstrue it; because we forget its practical origin and aim, its reference to the will-world. As a guide or plan to direct our way and determine our attitude in the will-world, its truth means its conformity to that end. The Church's zeal for any point of pure history, or science, or philosophy, is always *ultimately* in the interest of "eternal life;" of some point of the relationship of souls to God. Convince her that this interest is not threatened and she becomes indifferent at once.

In speaking of the "practical aim of religion," we seem to fall into the shallow heresy of "rationalism in religion," which denies all mystery in revelation, and admits nothing as divine truth whose bearing on rational ethics is not apparent. But this is to ignore the life of religion as distinct from the life of ethical conduct; it is to treat religion as simply the servant of morality, to make the prophet merely the ally of the moral philosopher and the magistrate. The "religionising" of conduct is not religion, but only one of its principal conditions and consequences. It is in the field of conduct that we work the work of God, and thus bring our wills into communion with His; but this will-communion is the end, of which conduct is but the occasion or means; and not conversely. We do not love in order to labour, but labour in order to love. This love, this sense of communion, is the very substance and basis of our spiritual being; our conduct is at best its manifestation, and belongs to our surface life.

If we love another we shall wish to know his will so far as it lies with us to perform it; but we shall also wish to know all we can about him, and not merely what he wants us to do; for it is by our knowledge of him that our love is fed and our union strengthened.

Love is not a part of conduct, but a spring or motive. It is that which acts. Hence in saying, as we may, that all revelation is directed to love and to the life of religion, we are in strict opposition to those who say that it is directed solely to conduct and to the "religionising" of life. Hence mysteries, which have no direct ethical value, bear most directly on love, which ever seeks a certain infinity and hiddenness in the object of its affection. A thoroughly comprehensible personality could have no attraction for us; it would afford no scope for the unitive effort in which love consists. There must be always a "beyond," a new territory to conquer, a new difference to overcome; for love is not a statical agreement, but a process of coming into agreement. Each personality is ever changing into something else; and no two could at any instant be quite the same. At best there is a harmony of dissimilars, and it is one that needs perpetual adjustment to keep pace with spiritual growth. It is neither what we seem to understand about God that feeds our love; nor the fact that He is infinitely beyond our understanding; but the fact that we can ever progress in knowledge and love, and always with a sense of an infinite "beyond." It is at the margin where the conquering light meets the receding darkness that love finds its inspirations. If we are forced to conceive Him human-wise, we know that the conception is but an idol or picture : that if He is all that, He is also infinitely more. To the savage He is but the biggest and strongest of men ; to the rationalist He is but the most intelligent and moral; to Faith He is the hidden Infinite, of which these are but the finite symbols.

But though God does not reveal Himself to us in the Christian religion merely as a model of good conduct; it remains true that all His revelation is directed to, and in some sense proceeds from, the life of Divine Love in the soul. "What! wouldst thou wit thy Lord's meaning in this thing? Wit it well, Love was His meaning. Who shewed it thee? Love. Wherefore shewed He it thee? For Love. Hold thee therein, thou shalt wit it more in the same. But thou shalt never wit therein other without end." These words, with which the anchoress Juliana, of Norwich, ends her revelations in the fourteenth century, are true of all revelation however intellectualised in form—were it even the creed of Athanasius. So far as it is from God's inspiration, it is a word to the heart and not to the head; and as such it must be criticised; it is an endeavour to find a mental and verbal expression of some new experience or intuition of that will-world of which love is the bond. Hence, though their immediate bearing on good conduct is not always apparent, the articles of the Creed, especially taken in their unity as one organic expression of God's relation to man, are plainly directed to the life of love, to determining more fully and completely our will-attitude in regard to God, and to the whole will-world as united with Him. Indeed, that Faith and Hope are but ministerial to Charity, as to the permanent substance and end of religion, is a truism.

That vague undirected love and worship of Truth and Goodness, which we might call the protoplasm or primary matter of spiritual religion, is first organised, defined, and intensified, when it finds its object in a personal will with which we can enter into relations of affection and sympathy; still more when it is conceived as the will of the All-Father and Creator, *i.e.*, of Him in whom all things live and move, and are; and when this mysterious nature is revealed to us in the likeness of our own, and shared by a plurality of persons, making a Divine love-bound society capable of entering into covenant with our collective humanity; and when an Eternal Son incarnate, utters God's love for man in the human language of devotion even unto death; and when a third Person of the Divine family is revealed as the sanctifier and consoler of the human spirit in its labour of self-development. And, similarly such dogmas as those concerning the sacraments, the communion of Saints, the forgiveness of sins, the resurrection of the body and life everlasting—to what are they all directed, but to the harmonising of our affections with the Divine Will, to the deepening and widening of charity, in other words—to Eternal Life?

VIII.

THE TRUTH OF BELIEFS.

IN its external expression a religion consists of a body of theological and ethical propositions, as well as of sundry rites, ceremonies, institutions, and disciplinary observances. As the rite or sacrament has its visible and spiritual side, its value as a fact in the world of appearances and its value as a fact in the will-world; so, I have implied, each ethical or theological statement is sacramental and belongs at once to the world of the natural understanding, and to the world of faith and spiritual reality. It is as to *faith* and *morals* (*i.e.*, as to spiritual and religious valuations) that the scriptures and traditions of the Christian Church claim to be divinely guided into all truth, as it were, by an unerring spirit or sentiment, which selects or casts aside such materials as are offered by the thought and language of each age and people for its embodiment—a spirit which, itself unchanged, changes the fashion of its outer garb to suit every variety of custom and tradition. That texture of philosophical, scientific, and historical beliefs, which the religious sentiment of Christianity has inspired and in which it has embodied itself, claims to be in harmony with the rest of human knowledge, of which it is but a part, and so far, to be true with the truth of the understanding; but its religious truth lies in "the spirit that quickeneth," in its fidelity to the facts of the will-world compared with which "the flesh," the merely mental value, "profiteth nothing." From every new ingathering of knowledge the same spirit can weave itself a living garment of flesh, not less, but more pliant to its purpose of self-manifestation than all previous garments.

The world of appearance, as we have said, is simply subordinate and instrumental to the real world of our will and affections in which we live the life of love and hate, and pass from one will-attitude to another in relation to other wills than our own. This will-life becomes religious as soon as we rise to a distinct knowledge of a Divine Will as the head and centre of the will-world. In this region truth has a practical and teleological sense—it is the trueness of a means to its end, of an instrument to its purpose; and like these truths it is to some extent conditioned by what we know and believe about its object. But this will-adjustment is the end of all such knowledge and belief, and constitutes its religious value. Hence the *religiously* important criticism to be applied to points of Christian belief, whether historical, philosophic, or scientific, is not that which interests the historian, philosopher, or scientist; but that which is supplied by the spirit of Christ, the *spiritus qui vivificat:* Is the belief in accord with, is it a development of, the spirit of the Gospel? What is its religious value? Does it make for the love of God and man? Does it show us the Father and reveal to us our sonship?

Such religiously true beliefs have been either created or shaped or selected under the influence of religious inspiration, that is, of the sacred enthusiasm kindled by some piercing intuition, some vivid perception of the realities of the will-world to which they correspond.

We may usefully distinguish a threefold truth or correspondence to reality in that organic body of beliefs known as the Christian creed. First, they may be viewed externally as woven into the tissue of our natural understanding, and as forming elements of our whole history and philosophy of the world—of our attempt to put things together coherently and to connect religion with the rest of our knowledge. Thus the existence and the nature of God, the immortality of the soul, the freedom of the will, may be viewed as constitutive elements of our philosophy; the birth, death and resurrection of Christ, as links in the chain of history.

Secondly, as a man's spirit and character may be revealed and known by his reading of history and by his view of the world and life, by the colour they derive from the glass through which he sees them, by the shape to which his receptivity moulds them, so the spirit of Christianity is revealed and known in the Creed. This truth of the Creed's correspondence to the spirit of

Christianity is only another aspect of its practical or "regulative" truth. It is by living in the light of these beliefs, by regulating our conduct according to them that we can reproduce and foster the spirit of Christ within ourselves. They furnish us with an effectual guide to eternal life.

Thirdly, a mere fiction may be practically serviceable in art or industry; and even the natural life of soul and body may be aided for a time and in particular cases by useful illusions. But no mere fiction, no pure illusion, no lie can be practically serviceable to life on an universal scale. For life depends on agreement with Nature; that is, on truth. Rogues and liars prosper just so long as there is a majority of honest men to lie to; but a community of rogues could not hold together; their theory of conduct is untrue to the nature of human society. Beliefs that have been found by continuous and invariable experience to foster and promote the spiritual life of the soul must so far be in accord with the nature and the laws of that will-world with which it is the aim of religion to bring us into harmony; their practical value results from, and is founded in, their representative value. Not indeed that the spirit-world can be properly represented in terms of the natural world. But as we can speak of thought in terms of extension, or of will in terms of mass and motion, on account of certain analogies between the two; so we can be sure that between the Christian understanding, or formulation of religion as embodied in the Creed, and the eternal realities of the spirit-world there exists a certain analogy whose precise nature is hidden just because we cannot compare its terms as we can those of thought and extension. And the reason of this assurance is found in the universally proved value of the Creed as a practical guide to the eternal life of the soul—a proof which is based on the experience not of this man or that, however wise or holy, but of the whole Christian people and of the Church of the Saints in all ages and nations, on the consensus of the ethical and religious *orbis terrarum*.

IX.

LEX ORANDI.

That "the rule of prayer is the rule of belief" (*lex orandi, lex credendi*) does not mean that every popular devotion rests on a sound dogmatic basis; or that even the most widely venerated relic is *ipso facto* genuine; or that we must believe *de fide* in the translation of the Holy House because there is a Mass in its honour. The maxim has reference to the prayer and the belief of the universal Church, of the whole body of the faithful in which the life of Christ is continued, in whose members collectively the spirit of Christ, the spirit of Charity, is spread abroad. "Prayer" is to be taken widely for the life of Charity, of Divine Love, of will-union with God and His Saints; "Belief" is to be taken for those conceptions of the nature and laws of the other world which are presupposed by Charity, which determine and characterise that Divine Love and give it its special tone and colour. In other words, a perfect penetration of the nature of Divine Charity and of the Christian spirit, would show us that this spirit of Charity was begotten and fed by those truths which find their expression in the Creed. More strictly it is begotten by a mysterious, abiding contact of the human soul with God; and the Creed is but the record of the gradual unravelling of the meaning of that experience through the collective spiritual labour of the Church, guided by the Spirit of Christ, into all truth. Not all at once, but by a slow evolution do the hidden implications of Divine Charity become explicit in the consciousness of the Church, according as the life of Christ lives itself out and exhibits its infinite potentialities in the life of His mystical body.

The Creed with all its legitimate developments is wrapt up in the Lord's Prayer which embodies the aims and aspirations of the human soul of Christ, and gives voice to His Love. If the "Our Father" is the criterion of all Christian prayer by which every spirit is to be tried; it is indirectly the criterion of every belief, just because prayer and belief are so inextricably intertwined. The affection which breathes forth the prayer cannot be fixed and communicated to others without some indication of the facts and truths that have kindled the affection; and these must be expressed, however roughly, in the conceptions of the mind. The fatherhood of God; the brotherhood of man; the kingdom of Heaven; the triumph of the Divine Will; Providence; Sin; Reconciliation; Deliverance; these and others are the ideas which beget, characterise and control the affection that utters itself in the Lord's Prayer; and of these ideas the Creed is the amplification and closer definition—a definition demanded not by mere theological curiosity, but by the very growth of the spirit of Love (in the collective Christian soul) to a greater explicitness and self-awareness. It is the Saints in virtue of their sanctity who have been the chief authors of this unfolding of the spirit of Christ and consequently, though perhaps indirectly, of those doctrinal expressions in which that unfolding has embodied itself.

They who best live the life, best know of the doctrine. Those beliefs that have been fashioned by pure theological curiosity, or by false piety, or by superstition, or in the interests of laxity or worldliness or avarice are local, ephemeral; and having no root they soon wither away. *Quod semper; quod ubique; quod ab omnibus* is the test—Beliefs that bring forth the fruit of holiness and charity more or less abundantly just in the measure that they are lived and practised; that do so with a certain universality, at all times, in all places, in all men, are thereby shown to be natural or true to the spirit of Christ, to be in harmony with the ultimate laws and realities of that supernatural world to which we are related by the life of Divine Love: "By their fruits you shall know them." Hence it is that no man can take his own subjective and separate experience as a sufficient test: "*Securus judicat orbis terrarum.*" If he is to develope a healthy individuality he must first appropriate and master what is common to all; he must correct his eccentricities by the teaching of the Church, that is, by the consensus of experts in the art of Charity; else he may be beguiled to eventual loss by a semblance of present gain, and mistake for healthy food what general experience has discovered to be a slow poison. For the spirit of Christ is in no man adequately and independently but only in virtue of his membership with the whole body of the faithful throughout which it is diffused. And indeed his subjective faith is nothing else than his obedience to the attraction which the spirit of Christ in the Church exercises upon the same spirit as latent in himself. Christ's sheep hear His voice because they are His already; because they are of His spirit. The more perfect Christ without them, the Christ of the Church's faith, cries out to the nascent Christ within them, spirit to spirit, with an importunity that cannot be resisted without violation of conscience. Not that the very earliest dawnings of the life of Divine Charity are exigent forthwith of all that explicit fulness of Christian belief which has fed the heroic love of the Saints; but that beginners in the life of Faith find inclusively in the Catholic Creed (as yet, too big and rich for their feeble powers of assimilation) those first roughly outlined notions of the Kingdom of Heaven which suffice for their present need: and that, just in the measure in which the spirit of Christ is truly developed in them, a more explicit belief will be felt as an exigency which the Church's fuller teachings can satisfy with all the security and authority of universal, as against individual, religious experience.

X.

THE DARK GLASS OF MYSTERY.

WE must now endeavour to exemplify the foregoing principles by applying them to some of the chief points of Catholic Christian belief so as to illustrate the manner in which the *Lex Credendi* or rule of faith has been determined and must be interpreted by the *Lex Orandi* or rule of prayer. We shall as far as possible consider these beliefs under their three-fold aspect (1) as truths of the understanding, (2) as truths of practical religious value, (3) as truths of that eternal order of being which eye hath not seen, nor ear heard, nor heart conceived save under the form of analogies.

But we must first insist more expressly on the fundamental fact that, just as our bodies are from the very beginning in felt relation to the bodily world, so our souls and wills are naturally, ceaselessly, in felt relation to the moral and spiritual world,—to that society of wills of which the Divine Will is the Source, the End, the Bond. In both cases we are forced instinctively to act or move in this direction or that, and by so doing to experience either ease or unrest according as the action harmonises or clashes with the interests of life and self-expansion. Through the recording, classifying and unifying of these experiences men have built up, gradually, by their joint labour, a plan or scheme of the whole world by which they can guide their action fruitfully and turn past experience to profit. This plan or scheme is the work of the rational understanding and finds its outer expression in language. Since it is only through our outward senses and through bodily signs that we can converse with one another, all our language and symbolism, all the forms of our understanding, are derived from the world of appearances, so that even our private and incommunicable feelings and desires have to be translated into terms of outward objects common to all, before we can speak of them; and it is only in this translated form that they are entered and registered in that scheme of our understanding which is essentially communicable, if not actually common, to all men. And with what result? That if we forget what we have done, and treat our symbolic descriptions of feelings and emotions as literal, we are landed in all sorts of absurdities when we try to understand them. Still more does this hold good of our higher inward experiences, our religious, social and moral affections and aspirations.

As soul and body make up one being, so do our inward and outward experiences make up one life, and so do the realms of spiritual reality — timeless and spaceless — and of material appearances make up one world. But this whole world of inward and outward experience has to be represented by our understanding and speech in terms of one (and that the lower) part, in terms of appearances; hence the inevitable confusion that attends our effort to explain spiritual experiences and realities and to weave them into one coherent system or scheme along with those of our bodily life; for, our mental reconstruction of the spiritual realm being necessarily built out of the same materials as our reconstruction of the physical realm possesses a far more indirect and imperfect truth-value than this latter. If then, the universe of physical Nature into which our bodies are woven and to which our bodily life adjusts us, exists representatively in our mind only as a rough diagram constructed or dotted-out from the fragmentary data of our narrow and momentary experiences, and barely serving the purpose of a practical guide to action; if Nature itself as presented in our limited experience is so infinitely less than what it would be presented in an unlimited experience, much more inadequate must be our mental understanding of the spiritual realm of which we have to speak and think in terms of Nature. If the former knowledge is necessarily inadequate, the latter must be mysterious as well as inadequate; it must abound in seeming anomalies and paradoxes.

As then our body is woven into the very tissue of the world of appearances of which each particle exerts a ceaseless influence on every other; as it is subject from the very first to a whole system of attractions and repulsions which it is the slow and painful task of science to unravel, set in order and unify; so too our will, through its immediate *rapport* with God, is knit into that spirit-world of which He is Source, Centre, and End; is subject to its influences in every conscious moment of life; and it is only by the accumulated results of religious reflection that the implications of these experiences are unfolded, sorted out, and built up into a mental reconstruction of the spirit-world. Revelations are but the epoch-making super-normal experiences of God-inspired prophetic souls, by which some unexplored tract of the Beyond is laid open to momentary observation, and furnishes the basis of a new law or generalisation which links incoherencies together and brings order out of previous confusion.

Just because God is the first, the deepest, the most continuous and all-permeating influence in our conscious life, He is the last clear result of this unravelling, unearthing process; the first thing given us in the order of "confused knowledge," He is the last to be known distinctly; the last, because of His very nearness, to be severed and pushed away from self, and viewed under the form of an object. Through the creature we can get to the Creator, through the finite to the Infinite. Good and evil first present themselves to our choice in those wills like our own with which we are in social relationship. From the glitter of these innumerable reflections we turn round to look up to their source in the heavens.

Thus we learn to distinguish between God as He is given in our experience and as He is represented in the constructions of our religious understanding; even as we do between Nature which presses and acts upon us as a whole, and Nature as known to us only in part—merely from the surface in contact—through the enigmatical constructions and symbols of science.

XI.

BELIEF IN GOD.

As we here use the term, religion is the will-attitude of the soul towards God considered as a Person, as that Sovereign Will which is the head, bond, and centre of the will-world. It is precisely under the aspect of goodness, or rather, since the will's ultimate object is never an abstraction, under the aspect of a Being in the act of loving, and willing, and causing, every possible kind of goodness and truth and beauty, that God is our principal will-object, the term of our unqualified love and worship and reverence. All else that we believe about Him is but an amplification of this aspect. So far as He belongs to that world of our understanding which systematises our experience with a view to converse and outward action, He is viewed as the First Cause, as Self-existent, Infinite, Eternal; or perhaps He is misconceived in some way or another, and some of His attributes distorted or denied. As the object of theological science we may *know* Him more or less; but we do not *believe* in Him. To believe in Him is to reckon with Him as a reality, and by free-choice to shape and adapt our inward and outward life with reference to that reality—yielding to it or resisting it.

The simplest can believe in Him, however incorrectly they may understand Him or apprehend all the philosophical implications of Necessary Being. To reckon with God as a reality, to enter into social relations with Him, does not necessarily mean leading a good life. The rebel who wilfully resists and defies authority confesses its reality by his defiance as much as he would by his submission. We do not beat the air or resist the void. Hostility is as real as friendship. Hence the distinction between belief and love is well founded and is consistent with the assertion that belief involves a practical attitude of the will, and does not stop short with a barren assent of the mind. "The devils believe and tremble;" their trembling is the very embodiment of their belief; for them God is not merely accepted by the mind, but is felt as an obstacle to the will.

The reasons and proofs that are commonly given for the existence of God are not always those that have historically given birth to the belief in His existence. Rather they are after-justifications of a belief that has risen independently of them, and represent an attempt to harmonise it with the rest of our understanding. Historically the belief has been fashioned by the religious needs of man's nature, and so far as it is true to that nature it must be justifiable by any philosophy that is true to the same. Truth is the same whether approached from the practical or the speculative side; what is really good, is true; what is true, is really the best.

In the measure that men have obeyed their inborn attraction towards the Ideal, feeling their way from one conception of the spiritual world to another according as this or that has proved its greater efficacy as a practical guide to inward life and growth, the notion of one supreme personal spirit, almighty, all-wise, all-holy as Source, Centre and End of the will-world has gained acceptance universally—*semper, ubique, ab omnibus;*

and has thereby proved its accord with the ultimate realities on which the laws of man's higher life are founded. The practical advantages and life-values of the great unifications of physical science are not more immediately apparent or indisputable than the moral and spiritual advantages resulting from the conception of the Infinite as being a personal Spirit or Will, giving unity of origin, centre, and aim to the otherwise aimless and chaotic multitude of finite wills; from the conception of this God as super-corporeal; as one rather than many; as just and holy rather than merely wise or powerful; as all-seeing, all-judging, rather than limited. Growing better, men have formed and approved these beliefs rather than their contraries; and approving them have grown still better, and have thus verified them experimentally.

It is plain that these beliefs are at first expressed simply and directly in the terms of things familiar to us, just as if they had been given us through our senses like the facts of history or science; and belonged to the world of appearances. But our mind, with its need of unity and coherence, cannot tolerate the confusion that would result from taking them in their simple literality, and at once sets about explaining them as analogously true in some way that will harmonise with the rest of our systematised knowledge.

It tells us that these beliefs will bring chaos into our understanding unless we are quite clear that, between the being and nature of God and that of all the creatures He has made there is no common measure, no relation of more and less, but an absolute difference *in kind;* that nothing can be said in just the same sense of Him and of any creature. This is what we mean by His infinity—not that He is indefinitely, endlessly, greater in measure and degree than anything we know in the way of being, unity, personality, spirit, knowledge, power, cause, will, goodness; but that He includes these in one simple absolute perfection in some way more different from them all than thought is from matter or than desire is from force.[1] In Him, what we call will is exactly the same thing as what we call knowledge, or being, or unity, or goodness; in us all these things are as distinct as possible and have nothing in common. He cannot strictly be grouped with anything

[1] See the note on analogy at the end of this chapter.

so as to be one of a class : but only by way of analogy. We call Him *a* spirit, *a* person, as if He were one of a number of such ; yet He is not one, or individual in the way that we are. He is a spirit only so far as this means that He is not corporeal ; He is a Person because most certainly He is not impersonal. What He *is* includes all that by which spirit excels body, and by which personality excels impersonality, and by which individuality excels indefiniteness and confusion. We do not even believe in *a* God, for this would imply a possible or conceivable multiplication of Gods : but only in God, for could we conceive Him adequately we should see that the idea of His replication was incoherent and absurd.[1]

[1] That it does not now strike us at once as inconceivable that the self-existent should be multiplied or extended is because the only "self" and the only "existence" that our understanding (as distinct from our intuition) knows is finite and limited and therefore can be conceived as multiplied. Again it is because we are forced to conceive God's existence in terms of our own and as of the same sort, that we do not at once see the *necessity* of His existence, the impossibility of His non-existence—our own sort of existence being merely contingent. It is only by roundabout reasoning that we are brought to see that there must be a higher kind of being than our own to account for our own; one whose existence is necessary and which cannot be measured by any finite measure.

That it is not so to us now, only shows that we cannot now think of Him, cannot make Him *an* object of our thought, cannot oppose Him to ourselves as another self, without at once putting Him into a class with other objects of our thought and so making Him finite in the image and likeness of creatures. This transformation is however necessary if we are to enter into social relations with Him—if we are to think of Him, love Him, pray to Him. As head and centre of the will-world He must be *represented* by us as *part* of that finite spiritual organism; as the First of Creatures; as making Himself man for our minds; as *a* power, *an* intelligence, *a* will indefinitely greater than, but of the same kind as, our own. Man cannot deal practically with what the heart of man has never conceived, with what is neither the self nor the not-self; with what is as distinct from him as the latter, yet quite differently distinct; as close to him as the former, yet quite differently close; with a relation that is necessarily *sui generis* and unknown to finite experience; he cannot deal with the Absolute in its absoluteness. The fiction of God's finitude and relativity is therefore a necessity of man's religious life. But the interests both of intellectual truth and of religion require us to recognise this fiction as such, under pain of mental incoherence on one side, and of superstition and idolatry on the other. For, to make God finite is to bring Him inside creation as its principal part or factor, just as a monarch is part of the society he governs; but to mistake this imaginary importation for a reality, to view God's immanence as that of a veritable *anima mundi*, part and parcel of the whole, revealed in Nature just as the soul is revealed in the body, would falsify all the calculations of our mind. Again, worship is not less idolatrous because the idol is greater than all other creatures put together. The reverence due to even the most marvellously gifted of our fellow-creatures differs altogether in kind from that due to the Giver on whose bounty we both alike are beggars; just as fraternal differs essentially from filial affection. This sentiment of adoring (latreutic) reverence owes its unique quality to the sense, however vague, of the absoluteness and infinitude which characterise its object, as being That which alone can satisfy the spiritual hunger which no idealisation of the finite, however great, could possibly satisfy. To lavish this sentiment on anything short of God is the very essence of idolatry. Yet if they cannot find bread men will eat earth in their vain efforts to stay the imperative cravings of their nature; for the appetite is there, as a vague uneasiness, from the very first, long before it arrives by way of experiment and failure at a distinct expression and understanding of itself and of its object.

The finite image, therefore, under which God is presented to us for the practical purposes of religion could not be universally useful to that spiritual life by whose exigencies it has been fabricated were it not grounded in the ultimate nature of things; were it not representative of the Infinite at least by way of analogy. There is a representative correspondence between a musical score and the music itself through which one stone-deaf from birth might be taught to produce effects, to exercise control, in that sound-world which has no direct place in his consciousness. Yet we cannot say that he knows nothing of the sound-world, that he has no evidence of its existence; we can only say that he does not know it in its own terms, but in terms of sight or touch. Though we know God's kind of being only in terms of our own, the Infinite only in terms of the finite, yet He is not therefore unknowable or unknown; nor is our action void of all effect in the order of Eternity.

Confusion as to this fundamental point is at the root of nearly all the difficulties we experience in endeavouring to reconcile the chief mysteries of faith with our natural understanding. Hence we have tried to put the matter clearly at the outset.

We have seen then how this popular notion of God as a personal spirit in our own image and likeness is true to the needs of our religious and moral life; and how it is true for the mind only so far as it is taken to represent the Divine order of being analogously in terms of the finite.

THE MEANING OF "ANALOGOUS."

As the analogous character of our notions about God has so often been misunderstood in an agnostic sense, I append here a brief *resumé*—which I have given elsewhere in an altered form—of the teaching of

St. Thomas Aquinas (*Summa Theol.* Pt. I. qq. 1 to 12) who, as the highest accredited exponent of dogmatism, can scarcely be accused of agnosticism.

Assuming that reason forces us to admit the existence of one necessary Being, all-wise, all-powerful, all-good, the first and all-sufficient cause of every finite perfection, I have implied that between these attributions (existence, being, unity, necessity, wisdom, goodness, power, "firstness," causality) as used of God and as used of creatures there is no common or identical measure, but only an analogy; that God is more than generically distinct from any finite being; that He is unthinkable save as the hidden synthesis of irreconcilables; we affirm that the synthesis exists, but of its precise nature we have no proper idea. What drives us to this affirmation is the necessity of believing that all finite perfections and advantages, however mutually exclusive, must be united and transcended in the simplicity of their common source. Owing to this absolute simplicity, what we call knowledge, goodness, power, etc., in God, are but aspects of exactly the same inscrutable thing or perfection. In us these qualities are incurably distinct; they can be magnified indefinitely without ever merging into one another. Hence, when we call God " Goodness," " Knowledge," or " Power," we mean something qualitatively diverse from our own goodness, knowledge, and power, which are for ever distinct from one another, and are not God. Between His goodness and ours there is not a mere arithmetic difference of more or less; nor yet one of added or subtracted qualities leaving a common generic element; but there is simple diversity or all-permeating difference.

When I speak of God as "goodness," I mean that as the ultimate simple source of that and of all perfections in creatures, He must possess it infinitely—not merely without limits of *degree*, but without those limits of *kind* that in us make goodness separable, and separate from knowledge, power, existence, etc. Could I conceive God properly and not analogously I should see that He was, and that He was not, all at once, Goodness, Knowledge, Power, etc.; that Deity was a diverse perfection from them all, yet including and transcending them all. To say that "He is good and not-good" does not mean that He is good and bad, but that the simple synthesis of all perfections cannot be properly described by the name of only one. Since what I call Goodness in God might just as well, under another aspect, be called Being or Wisdom, it is plain that Goodness is said of Him in a non-proper or analogous sense. And yet it is equally plain that it conveys real information about God over and above what is conveyed by the terms Wisdom and Being; and that by the accumulation of such analogous predications we approximate towards the ever unattainable comprehension of Deity.

Between such things as thought and extension which belong to totally different genera there can be no identical predication founded on community of content. We can only find analogous resemblances, and speak of one, almost poetically, in terms of the other. Again, though their inner character is wholly diverse they agree in being each of them an object of thought, a "something" possessing a certain analogous unity, truth, value, etc., from which certain very abstract and barren conclusions may be drawn from one case to the other. So barren and abstract or at best poetical or metaphorical would be our notions of God derived from creatures were He simply in a different category or genus from the finite; but if He is infinitely further in one sense, He is infinitely nearer in another. His being is not related to man's, as that of thought to that of extension, or as that of desire to that of physical force. He is not known merely as "something," but as the root and source of everything as immanent no less than transcendent—a relation which does not exist between finite things of wholly disparate categories. The relation between branch and branch is different from that between branch and root. Our knowledge of God is therefore not limited to those attributes which belong to every term of thought, to every " something," as such, but embraces, without limitation of degree *or kind*, whatever perfection of content is predicable of any possible thing or term of thought. So understood, the scholastic doctrine of analogy steers successfully between the Scylla of illegitimate dogmatism and the Charybdis of Spencerian agnosticism.

XII.

BELIEF IN FREE-WILL.

BELIEF in the freedom of the will and belief in the immortality of the soul are so closely bound up with religion as to demand here a short consideration. Together with the belief in God, they constitute the *Credo* of what is sometimes called, rather inaccurately, "Natural Religion." They are both given to us primarily by the experiences of our inner life, which they are found to explain and to foster. Historically, it is their regulative and practical truth that is first apparent to us—their life-value and their harmony with the nature of the soul. Always, everywhere, in every one—*Semper, ubique, ab omnibus*—these beliefs, wherever they are established, go hand in hand with the higher development of man's moral and spiritual life, private and social. This universality of their practical truth warrants a belief in their correspondence to the inmost and deepest realities of the spiritual order which they represent, not properly but analogously, in terms of the world of appearances. If they are to be harmonised with our understanding it must be by a clear recognition of their analogous character, and of the limits within which they are true under that materialised form which they spontaneously take in our mind.

It may be at once objected that the fullest vigour of moral and spiritual life has often been attained by those whose creed or philosophy denies the freedom of the will: who regard it as rigidly determined by Nature or by God. But the beliefs we are dealing with are the spontaneous suggestions of experience in their crude form before the understanding has endeavoured to reconcile them with itself. All admit that the first suggestion of experience is that in certain matters we are free and responsible, worthy of praise or blame, as being the ultimate originators of certain effects; and that in many other matters we are worthy of neither praise or blame, being but passively determined by causes outside ourselves. Those who, failing altogether to reconcile this belief in freedom with their understanding, reject it as an illusion, are in theory "determinists" or "fatalists," but none the less in practice they obey the so-called illusion and admit its practical utility. Treating freedom thus as a fact or reality they still "believe" in it, and owe their moral and religious vigour not to their theoretical denial but to their practical belief. Our personal experience will show us that, in any given matter of conduct, a belief in our freedom, in our power to act, is a necessary condition for the exercise of such power; we never attempt the possible if we believe it to be impossible; we give up trying and yield ourselves passively to the forces that play upon us. The "determinists" have often tried to show that their theory *ought not* to limit life's energy in any way; and possibly it would not, in the case of one who had persuaded himself on the point philosophically. But viewed as a belief, and not as a theory; as it presents itself simply to the mind, not as sophisticated by after-reflection, the denial of man's freedom, whether in general, or in some particular matter, works as disastrously as the belief in it works fruitfully. We cannot then doubt as to which belief is more consonant to the ultimate realities of the spiritual world, or allow the perplexities it offers to the understanding to shake our conviction for a moment.

But what is the root of these perplexities? It lies in this; that our will belongs to the world of realities, whereas our understanding can represent things only in terms of the world of appearances, of things that are seen and touched, that are measured by time and space—of things that are moved passively. A moment's reflection will convince us of the truth that no single instance of *action* is offered to our senses in the world around us. The horse moves; the cart follows; we call the first "action" but we really mean that it is the *result* of the horse's action which is itself inferred and not seen. Strictly, the movement of the horse's limbs, like any other movement in outward Nature, is as much a passive result as is the movement of the cart. One, and one only, instance of action is directly known to us, and that is the action of our own will: every other action is simply inferred and not seen. Seeing effects like those that result from our own action we instinctively suppose them due to a similar cause. But we *represent* and *understand* action necessarily under the figure of a passive movement which precedes some other movement that is rigidly connected with it, as the movement of the cart is with that of the horse. Forgetting that this is but a figure or symbol, we turn back and think of our own will and action as a movement of which our spirit is not productive but receptive, and we ask : How is it caused ? If by ourselves, then this causing of it is a previous action which presents the same difficulty : and so on for ever. If not by ourselves, how are we responsible? We fancy the alternative is between a pair of scales that obeys the weights passively ; and one that moves itself miraculously regardless of the weights. Passivity and determinism are all that is given us in the world of appearances ; and so long as we try to understand action and freedom in terms of that world, we shall be forced to deny them in theory unless we remember that our representations are only analogous and symbolic of the real world. The very words " freedom," " self-determination," or any others we can coin, are rife with snares if we take them literally. And yet our free action is better and earlier known to us than anything else and is presupposed to all possibility of further knowledge—for it is in our action, and as acting, that we know ourselves; we cannot go behind it in thought, or compare it to anything else, or classify it among the contents of our understanding. Action, the exercise of freedom, is the exercise of our spiritual existence. It is as with "knowing." We have to speak and think of "knowing" in terms of its conditions or objects. We know an object from its picture, symbol, or representation; but this too is an object; and how is it known? "Knowing" cannot be understood because it is presupposed to all understanding; we cannot get behind it since, like "willing," it is but an aspect of our spiritual self, and we cannot get behind ourselves.

If then we cannot represent our own action, than which nothing is better known to us, in the terms of our understanding except by way of analogy, how shall we hope to represent that mysterious, unknown influence which God exercises continually in, over, and through our action, as the First Mover in every movement? If we call it "will" or "action," we seem at once to make our own will or action its passive result in us; something done *to* us but not *by* us. Hence, we must remember that it is not an action or cause of the same order as ours, but of an infinite or incommeasurable order; that action is said of God analogously; that it is only another name for what He *is* when viewed as the presupposition of all action. Our action depends not on anything He literally *does*, but on the fact that He *is*.

Thus that naïve belief in our freedom, which is proved true to the ultimate realities of the spiritual order by its universal fruitfulness in practice, can be brought into harmony with the reflex understanding as soon as its analogous character is duly recognised. Prior to and independently of this, the belief is true to the practical exigencies of life: true thereby to the realities which are at the root of those exigencies, but more or less false to the world as re-constructed in the scheme of our understanding out of materials borrowed eventually from the realm of determinism.

XIII.

BELIEF IN IMMORTALITY.

UNLIKE the belief in free-will, that in the immortality of the soul is not explicitly presupposed from the first beginnings and in every act of the life of religion. Yet the further development of that life makes it plain that these first beginnings are inexplicable unless immortality *be* a truth; although the express acknowledgement of this truth be not needed till a later stage of spiritual growth. This acknowledgement becomes a necessity of religious life in the measure that men realise that there is and can be but one God over all, who is a just and righteous God rendering to every man according to his own personal merits, and therefore rectifying in some other state of existence the patent inequalities and injustices of a world where the wicked flourish like bay-trees and when the just man dieth no one taketh it to heart; and again, in the measure that the absolute worth and the inexhaustible capacities of each individual soul are realised in a way to make intolerable and irreconcilable with any intelligible estimate of God's wisdom, goodness, and love, the supposition that this mortal life offers an adequate environment for man's spiritual development, or can be anything more than a preliminary and embryonic stage of his history—a time when the seed is sown that bears, no doubt, a ratio to the future harvest; when foundations are laid that in some way fix the character of the future structure; when a path is chosen that must be traversed hereafter to its infinite consequences. In short, when the spiritual life of friendship and will-union with God comes to be recognised as an end in itself, and *the* end to which every other life-interest must be subordinate, the belief in the eternity and imperishableness of that life becomes an axiom of religion.

No valid argument indeed can be based on the universal prevalence of that purely animal longing for life and shrinking from death which is but another phase of the brute instinct of self-preservation; on the wish for an endless continuance of present conditions. Only those who live most worthlessly and frivolously, can fancy that they desire or would be contented with an eternity of the same routine of inanity that fills the days and years of their life; those who feel no torturing limitations, no pent-up expansiveness. For indeed it is only a fancy. Physical appetite unsatisfied seems limitless in its cravings; but satiety comes at last even for the greediest; and the days wherein a man shall say: "I have no pleasure in them." "Only to cheap curiosity," says Münsterberg, "can it appear desirable that the inner life, viewed as a series of psychological facts, shall go on and on. . . . It would be intolerable for seventy years: who would desire it for seventy million years? . . . It is like the thought of endlessness in space; if we were to grow endlessly tall, physically almighty, would our life be more worth living?" It is as a postulate, not of physical but of spiritual life that the belief in immortality grows more imperative with every development of that life—a life whose progress is not that of monotonous quantitative prolongation but that of ceaseless expansions and transformations into something qualitatively different and better.

The history of the belief and of its variations establishes this connection with an irresistible solidity.

If Bouddhism be instanced as an older and more wide-spread religion than Christianity and yet one which regards a future life as a calamity from which men should seek eventual deliverance by flight and voluntary self-limitation, it must be remembered that it is a religion which believes in no God, which denies the worth of life; that is without faith, without hope; intent only on finding escape from sorrow in silence and extinction; in short, that it is not a religion at all, in the sense in which the term is used in these pages; but only an ethical system, a way of life, or rather of death, with whose pessimism the denial of immortality were perfectly consonant.

The worship and service of God merely as the protector of one's people and nation or as the dispenser of temporal blessings and chastisements does not, of course, postulate a belief in immortality; but so far as higher motives are positively excluded from such worship it cannot be viewed as an exercise of the inner life or of religion in the spiritual sense of the term, since it is subordinated wholly to the interests of the outer life.

"*Let us eat and drink for to-morrow we die*" expresses in its grossest form that paralysis of spiritual life which issues in the case of most men from a decisive denial of immortality. Many there are for whom such denial is not apparently inconsistent with a devotion to the ideal and with high ethical development: yet it may be questioned whether in such cases there be not some sub-conscious hoping against hope, some secret revolt of the religious sense against the abstract reason; or at the very least a belief that somehow, somewhere, good and evil, truth and lie, fair and foul, are fraught with eternal consequences for humanity. So naturally inwrought is this conviction of conscience that it needs to be continually and explicitly denied if it is not to re-assert itself in every act of our will. Let us once realise and feel that Humanity is as mortal as the individual—dust from dust, returning to the dust, be it a mountain of dust or a handful—let us once be quite sure that when this spinning ball of earth comes to a standstill or is shattered to atoms, the history of man's life upon it will be as a tale told by an idiot, what will idealism be but a bubble that is pricked, an illusion whose spell is broken? The spiritual life is eternal or nothing.

> . . . If Death were seen
> At first as Death, Love had not been,
> Or been in narrowest working shut,—
> Mere fellowship of sluggish moods.[1]

"Always, everywhere, in all men," this belief in the eternal destiny of the individual soul has proved itself fruitful in an immense deepening, strengthening and enrichment of the spiritual life; and has thereby proved itself true to the nature and laws of that real world with which that spiritual life puts us *en rapport*. Its practical truth must therefore be rooted in its truth as a representation of the invisible world.

Plainly it represents that world more or less in terms of this, and so far possesses a merely analogical or equivalent truth. Its demands will be satisfied in some higher and

[1] *In Memoriam*, xxxv.

better form, not in the precise form of our materialised conceptions. The materiality of these conceptions is inevitable because all our language is borrowed from natural things, their measurements, relations and properties. We are bound to think of the future life and world as etherialised continuations of these present; of eternity as time indefinitely prolonged; and of the soul as an attenuated, filmy replica or shadow of the body, as a something that enters it, leaves it, goes up and down, flits here and there. Between the very rudest and the most cultivated picturings of the soul and of its future state, there is a difference only of degree in point of materialism. Not only must we perforce think of the spirit or *real* self, in terms of the body or *apparent·* self, but we must also think of its timeless and indivisible action in terms of these appearances to which its action relates. We divide its knowing and its willing and feeling into groups and series of separate acts answering to the fragments and moments of our brain-movement, and thus ascribe to it a sort of life that is essentially bodily and mortal— much as, in spite of science, our imagination

H

persists in ascribing to the sun those movements that belong only to the still-seeming earth. Under this illusion we can think of spiritual immortality merely as an endless prolongation of our nerve-and-brain life. But take the spirit out of the world of appearances and the question as to its mortality becomes vacant of all sense.

It is by such reflections on the merely analogous representative-value of our spontaneous notions about the soul, its immortality and its future state, that the understanding is enabled to harmonise these notions with its re-construction or putting-together of things in general.

Beliefs that are proved true to the laws of man's highest life and thereby to the ultimate realities of the spiritual order cannot be wholly in conflict with an understanding that is true to Nature. It must at least find place for them even if it cannot always demonstrate them; it cannot exclude them without stultifying its whole *raison d'être*. For the understanding is but an instrument fashioned by the will to serve as a guide to life and action. It is shaped, not out of nothing, by the co-ordination and harmonising of just those very spontaneous notions and beliefs that experience has proved fruitful of life. If this co-ordination can be effected only through the exclusion of the chief of them, the work must be broken up and begun all over again. The claims of certain beliefs are stronger than those of any system that would exclude them.

XIV.

BELIEF IN THE BLESSED TRINITY.

THE doctrine of three persons in one God was first revealed in substance by Christ and was developed to greater distinctness by the faithful under the influence and guidance of the Spirit of Christ. It is a conception of the Divinity which shapes, characterises and expresses that particular quality of supernatural love towards God and man that burned as a fire in the Heart of Christ and was thence kindled over the face of the earth among His disciples. It gives a new and far more explicit constitution to that willworld in which our inner life of Grace is lived, determining more exactly the nature of its source, end, and centre, and, by consequence, of our relations to it, and to one another through it. Like every other doctrine of the Christian faith, this of the Trinity is the creation of love and life; it was felt and lived before it was expressed in terms of the understanding. In it Christ and the Church have but unfolded more fully the secret implications of Charity—have, as it were, accounted for it. In its feeble beginnings Grace was in man as a vague feeling whose nature and efficient source were but dimly defined; not till it gathered to its utmost force and intensity in the human soul of Christ was its origin clearly revealed to man's mind as a Trinity of divine persons, Father, Son and Spirit.

We cannot love what we do not know, any more than we can think without something to think about. But we can know a thing simply as that which attracts or repels us in a certain way, in a certain direction; we can know it in, and with, that very attraction or repulsion long before we can make any sort of representation of it in our mind. And thus in the movements of Grace, in the attraction to good, in the repugnance to evil, we know God and the Blessed Trinity long before we shape any image of them in our thought.

If the idea of God, as given us by the requirements of religious experience, needed to be explained as analogous in order to be harmonised with our general understanding and scheme of existence, the notion of three persons in God demands yet further adjustment, so as to stand together with our belief in the unity of God. With this belief it seems to conflict just so far as the analogous character of our knowledge of God is forgotten or misunderstood. The polytheistic conception of the Divine as a multitude of persons constituting a society or government of a very human type, although it saves a part of the truth that is lost in unitarianism, belongs on the whole to a religion far lower than that monolatry which, without denying the existence of other gods, chooses one as its supreme and only object of worship. A further step towards truth is attained when the very existence of other gods is denied or when they are degraded to a lower order of being. But monotheism has not reached its full expression till the inherent impossibility of more than one God is clearly recognised; till His unity is no longer conceived to be like that of the sun, or of the physical universe, or of any thing which *might* be multiplied as being one of a possible, if not actual, number;

but is divested of every sort of materiality and finitude. But the unity of what *we* mean by a "person" is its distinctness from other possible or actual persons; hence the unity of the Divine Nature is not that of a person. The unitarianism of what is called "Natural Theology" always forgets that God can be called "*a* person," "*a* spirit" only by way of analogy, and that the analogy affects the grammatical article as well as the substantive; that because God is by nature one and personal it does not follow that He is one person and not many. The oneness of personal distinctness and the oneness of impossible multiplication of nature are absolutely different ideas; we cannot argue from one to the other.

The very same necessity which forces us to ascribe to God the perfection without the limitation of our own personality and to call Him "a person" and "a spirit"; which forbids us to think of Him as corporeal or impersonal, forces us no less to ascribe to Him the perfection of our social life as members of a community of persons. This necessity of thought was rudely satisfied by polytheism, nor was it felt so keenly as long as the one God was conceived more or less humanwise, and as on a level with rational creatures over whom he ruled as monarch; for the monarch is part of the social organism and enters into its life. But when reflection had corrected these imperfect conceptions, it left men with the deistic idea of an unipersonal God reigning in solitude and cold isolation from eternity to eternity. It is to the correction of this idea that the Christian doctrine of the Trinity comes as a relief. If it is given us by revelation and not by the necessities of thought; yet far from encountering an obstacle, it finds a vacancy ready for itself in the purer conception of monotheism. Morality and society are correlative notions; if by analogy God is a moral being He must in the same sense be a social being. God is Love—*Deus est Caritas*—and love is a relation between persons. "Love" "Person" "Society"—all these are names of that which God *is;* all are said of Him analogously and yet with a certain truth and correspondence to the infinite reality whose precise value must remain inscrutable to our finite minds. Only so far as we secretly and unconsciously conceive God as finite can the doctrine of the Trinity offer the slightest *positive* difficulty to our understanding. A mystery it will ever remain, a datum of faith and revelation, a practical truth of the inner life, an exigency of Christian love, but not a necessity of philosophical thought.

XV.

BELIEF IN GOD'S FATHERHOOD.

"God so loved the world that He gave His only-begotten Son," is a saying that speaks straight to the heart of the simplest, however untheological be his conception of that mysterious Sonship. The gift of no mere son by adoption, of no creature however sacred and full of grace, could convey to us so deep a sense of the Divine love, as is conveyed to us by this gift on the part of the Eternal Father of that co-equal Son begotten of His very substance. Had He suffered but the holiest and greatest of His created sons to die for us, we could have conceived a sort of love among men greater than the love of God; and even had God sacrificed Himself for us, He would have seemed to have given less than in giving us His Son—for what father would not give himself rather than his son?

This aspect of Divine love is the special feature of the Christian revelation. "Father, I have glorified Thee on earth; I have finished the work Thou gavest Me to do; I have declared Thy name (that is Thy name or nature as Father) to the men whom Thou gavest Me."[1] And St. Paul sums up the fruit of Christ's mission saying: "We have received the spirit of the adoption of sons whereby we cry: Abba, Father." With us, fatherhood means a title to reverence and love founded on a certain authorship, care and protection. When St. Paul says that all paternity in Heaven and earth is named after the divine archetypal fatherhood, he does not mean that, first knowing this latter we then recognise its reflection in the former; but that we should consider the highest ideals of finite paternity unworthy the name, could we only realise the absoluteness of our dependence on that Infinite Love which breathes us into being, and in which we live and move and are. Merely as Creator, as Providence, as all-permeating giver of life and movement both in body and soul, as one on whose abiding thought and

[1] John xvii.

affection we depend as do rays of light or heat on the source from which they stream, God claims from us that unique sentiment of sonship towards Himself and of brotherhood towards all our fellow-creatures in their several degrees of creaturehood which might seem to be the very sum and substance of religion. Yet the Christian Creed (unlike rational theology) looks on this relation of merely natural creatorship or fatherhood as something only hypothetical—something that might have been, but which never actually was. For centuries prior to certain heretical negations the Church never had occasion to advert to such an hypothesis at all in any explicit way. She had assumed that from the first and throughout, what we might call God's creative "co-operation" with man, and with the whole world in man's interest, had been of an immeasurably higher kind than what was needed by the nature of things; that all His workings in and for man's soul had been directed to uniting it with Himself in a way beyond all that man's spiritual necessities strictly required; that the Eternal Life for which man had in fact been created was really a sort of "grace"—an *undue* entering into the life of the Eternal; an adoption into the Divine Society or Family of the Father, Son and Spirit. Thus God's action in the will-world as *de facto* constituted is, both in its aim and in its inherent quality, other than what it would have been in such a merely possible world as rational theology deals with; and in virtue of this action the whole dispensation is said to be "supernatural," not as co-existing with, or superimposed on, but as substituted for, the natural that might have been.[1]

The religious value of this conception of the order of Grace, the peculiar tone and

---

[1] From this it will be clear that the supernatural order of Grace does not as such, *interfere* in any way with the laws of physics or psychology. The difference is, not in the structure or function of the creature—not in the musical instrument, but in the handling of the musician, in the measure of skill he chooses to put forth. Contrasted with the world that might have been, this *de facto* world would perhaps be observably different; but, historically speaking, the supernatural is "natural" to the world as man has always known it, and harmonises with its laws. Had the sun's light been miraculously doubled from the first we should never have suspected the miracle; the very uniformity of the phenomenon would have robbed it of its miraculous character. So it is that the order of Grace is supernatural but not *per se* miraculous; it cannot clash with the observed uniformities of our experience.

gave He power to become the sons of God." In this mysterious relation of sonship man was created; from this he fell; to this he was restored through Christ; created, fallen, redeemed, he has been always the subject of a super-natural dispensation;—the natural that might have been, is mere hypothesis.

That this way of taking things—of reconciling the interests of thought with those of religion—has been fruitful in love to God and man, and productive of a vast deepening and expansion of spiritual life the Saints of Christianity, the specific character of Christian sanctity, bear the witness of experience. The combination of the sense of man's nothingness before God's infinitude (which was lost to more childish religions), with the sense of man's supernatural elevation to companionship with God (which mere theism lacks) results in that strange blending of awful reverence and familiar tenderness, in that lowly confidence, that daring love, which is so peculiarly characteristic of Christian sanctity: —*Audemus dicere: Pater noster.*

Between the mystery of Grace and the general conceptions of the understanding there can be little or no positive conflict from the nature of the case. Still less does belief in the supernatural necessarily involve any observable or even secret breach in the uniformity of Nature. Yet if reason cannot demonstrate the existence of the order of Grace, its perplexities and disturbances point to that or some similar explanation of their origin. If Faith did not give us this solution we should have to forge some hypothesis for ourselves to solve the riddle of human history. Finally, from the proved practical fruitfulness of the belief, from its evident correspondence to the laws of spiritual life "always, everywhere, in every one" just in the measure that it is realised and followed out in action, we infer its fundamental truth as representing analogously and in terms of appearances the world of invisible reality.

XVI.

BELIEF IN GOD'S OMNIPOTENCE.

To the rudimentary religious sense God is presented as Power rather than as Wisdom, Righteousness or Love; or if at all as Wisdom, it is only because craft and skill multiply power. In his struggle for life against Nature, man seeks to control and utilise those unknown natural forces that else may destroy him. Before he begins to recognise Nature as a sort of mechanism whose laws may be learnt by observation, and while he as yet views every event as the free choice of some governing will or wills like his own, he puts his hope in an appeal to that will, rather than in his own endeavours guided by an understanding of Nature; he prays to his God as he would pray to his more powerful fellow-man. But this prayer is not in the interest of his inner, but of his outer life; will-union and friendship with the deity is not viewed as the chief end of life, but only as a means to other advantages. The object of Hope, of Prayer viewed strictly as an exercise of religion, is the inner life of will-union with God, its difficulties, doubts, struggles, defeats, victories—"Grace and Glory," that is, Love and the consummation of Love. Hence Christ bids us: Seek first the kingdom of God and His righteousness, leaving the rest to Providence; He forbids solicitude as to food, raiment and those needs of our outer life which the heathen demand from their gods. The Good Spirit, the Gift of God— for this we are to ask, and seek, and knock. If aught else be asked for it must be only so far as it seems to us a condition of this, and with such a submission to the divine judgment as He exemplified when He prayed: "*If it be possible* let this chalice pass from Me." Our Heavenly Father knows that we need these outer things and we do best to leave them silently to His care, reserving all our prayer-energy for the one thing needful. Thus in the Lord's Prayer we are taught to pray for no more than is needful and sufficient for the day, and not to take thought for the morrow. The words "Give us this day our daily bread" are less a petition, than an expression of trustful indifference as to the temporal needs of the future.

As a truth of religion, as the foundation of Hope, as the motive of Prayer, the omnipotence of God is to be understood relatively to the supernatural end of man, the kingdom of Heaven, the ultimate triumph of the Divine Will. So far, and no further, the belief is an exigency of the spiritual life. The metaphysical conception of the absolute infinitude of God's power is the fruit of mental speculation, not of practical life. It is enough for the soul to believe that all things, howsoever seemingly adverse, work together for the good of those who love God; that nothing, neither life nor death nor any other creature, can separate us from the love of God; that He can turn water into wine; weakness into strength; sorrow into joy; loss into gain; sin abounding into grace superabounding; that "with Him all things are possible" and every obstacle superable, in the interests of His ultimate victory over the hearts of men. Such a faith is universally necessary and conducive to the vigour and expansion of the moral and spiritual life and is therefore true to reality.

Yet the inner life of our will is so conditioned by, and dependent on, the outer life of the body that God's omnipotence in the order of Grace implies a similar omnipotence in that of Nature: "Your Heavenly Father knoweth that you have need of these things." Prayer for temporal favours that is not implicitly a prayer for grace or that is not at least made with a complete subordination of every interest to the one thing needful, is no doubt as superstitious as the magic by which the savage seeks to compel the power of his gods to his own profit; still, when duly conditional and submissive, prayer for external favours is universally considered to be a legitimate exercise of faith: "If it be possible," says Christ: "let this chalice pass from Me; yet not as I will but as Thou wilt."

God's omnipotence over Nature and in the realm of appearances is necessarily conceived by us in terms of our own power in that realm. We can think of and desire various alterations in the arrangement of the world, and within certain limits we can effect them —for the attitude of our will is one of the factors of the situation. The limits of our power are determined partly by the extent to which we understand or misunderstand the mechanism of Nature with its uniformities of grouping and sequence; partly by the inherent capabilities of that mechanism. No degree of skill in the performer can overcome the necessary limitations of the instrument. Thinking of God man-wise, we give Him the omnipotence of perfect knowledge and skill in the use of Nature. Furthermore, as the author of Nature, as the maker of the instrument, we ascribe to Him the power of miracle, *i.e.* of effecting every inherently possible change in its structure and laws. That He cannot make hills without hollows is no limitation of His omnipotence, nor that He cannot exercise His power in any way inconsistent with His wisdom, goodness and love, since in Him they are all identical. He can do every-*thing*, but a contradiction or absurdity is not a thing but a nothing.

But in all this way of thinking man is made the measure of God; the finite, of the

Infinite; God is brought inside creation as its organic head, its principal factor; as *a* cause, *a* will, *an* agency co-operant with, albeit sovereign over, other causes, wills and agencies. Of that Power which is another name for Being, which effects by *being* and not by *doing*, we can have no proper, but only an analogous, conception.

The religious implication which underlies the spiritual man's instinctive prayer to God for temporal things is the truth of the absolute dependence of Nature upon God; the denial of that fatalism which views Nature as a blind self-existent mechanism which God can manage and circumvent within limits, but which may evade His providence or thwart the designs of His love for a time, or even finally. Prayer implies that the whole thing is in His hands; that it is the creation of loving wisdom and is ministerial to Love.

"Though He should slay me yet will I hope in Him;" ruthlessly, brutally, blindly the law-bound mechanism seems to grind on for all man's impotent tears and cries for pity; and yet an invincible faith in Goodness as its Alpha and Omega bids him still weep and cry and pray—not as one who despairingly clutches at space in his fall, but as one who lays hold of that solid rock of reality on which his moral and spiritual life is built.

In a lawless world of absolute irregularity and caprice we could not live for a day; and our power of life and self-government is measured by the extent to which we can recognise the universal prevalence of law. As we grow from childhood to maturity in spiritual wisdom, we feel that universal order must make for that divine and universal good to which we should desire to offer ourselves in sacrifice, certain that, in the end, what is best for all will be best for each; we feel that much egoism is implied in the desire for dispensations and disturbances in our favour regardless of their wide-reaching consequences for others; we care less, nay, we fear more, to dictate to God in our own interest, and prefer to leave ourselves passively in His hands, not in a spirit of fatalism and doubt, but in a spirit of faith and confidence. We realise also that there is a prayer of presumption which is but a lazy evasion of the duty of vigilance and of the use of natural means that are to hand; a prayer which enervates and demoralises.

But we should be untrue to the laws of the spiritual life and to their eternal foundations were we so to exaggerate the reign of law in the realm of appearances as to deny all external causality to prayer. The fact, and the mode of its operativeness, are two different considerations. Of the latter we have analogous but no proper conceptions. That men's beliefs and desires and purposes are effective in the world of appearances and are factors of the situation around us is undeniable. So-called "Faith-cures," moral and physical, and many other kindred phenomena are confessedly within the established order of things and involve no interference with uniformity that ought to falsify our expectations or bring confusion into our life. That faith in God and prayer to God should under due conditions and within certain ill-defined limits be effective of alterations in the realm of appearances presents no *a priori* difficulty whatever, and is, like the rest, a matter of experience. Much that is alleged in the way of verification may be set aside by criticism, but a substantial residuum remains to justify the invincible instinct of religion. The notion that the real causality of prayer in the world of appearances necessarily or usually implies miracle is due only to confusion of thought.

XVII.

BELIEF IN GOD'S GOODNESS AND WISDOM.

(1.)

By God's goodness we mean His loving-kindness towards all His creatures so far as they are capable of any sort of happiness or unhappiness. A good man is one who finds his own happiness in the happiness of others. This benevolence is the effect or property, but not the substance, of his goodness; it is the sign of that in which his own goodness consists. "Goodness is self-diffusive"—a sun that radiates its light and warmth and communicates its own nature as far as possible to everything within the sphere of its influence. A good man desires the perfection and happiness of every conscious being in its own kind and measure; and this, in the case of spiritual beings, will show itself in like benevolence of loving-kindness on their part towards others, so that fire is kindled from fire and spread abroad over the earth.

Men did not always think it necessary to attribute this universal goodness to God; they thought of Him as friendly to themselves and to their friends (with certain excusable reserves of selfishness), and as hostile to their enemies. But with their own moral growth in goodness came the religious necessity of conceiving Him as infinitely better than the best of men, as universal Father and Lover of all, as making His sun to shine on the evil and the good and sending rain on the just and the unjust, as loving His enemies, blessing those that curse Him, doing good to those that hate Him, as caring for the birds of the air and the flowers of the field with a tenderness whose measure is His own greatness rather than their littleness.

This belief is an imperative exigency of the spiritual life in its higher phases—a God less kindly than the kindest of men and who could look with pleasure or indifference on the least suffering of the least creature could not be an object of worship. We should feel ourselves superior to him; nor could we pray to such an one in our troubles and sorrows with that absolute confidence and resignation which Christ has taught us. Not only does this belief grow with and from our spiritual growth, but it re-acts in accelerating that growth; it presents our own goodness to us as a manifestation of the indwelling Will of God in our souls, as a duty no less than an impulse; as an impulse to be fostered, no less than followed.

The conception of God as a Spirit endowed with an infinite measure of this sort of goodness must therefore have some analogous representative value in relation to the eternal order of reality in order to account for its universal correspondence to the natural laws of the spiritual and moral life.

But when we come to reconcile it with the world of outward experience as presented in our understanding, we seem to encounter insuperable difficulties in what is called "the Problem of Evil." To state this problem in its appalling dimensions, to criticise one by one the futile solutions that have been suggested would fill volumes. If our Faith in God's loving-kindness has to wait for a solution of this world-wide, world-old enigma it will have to wait for ever.

"Nature shrieks against our creed" as long as we consider Nature apart from man, the object without reference to the subject, the body as sundered from the soul, the members as torn from the head. Human goodness offers us the only solid argument for Divine: "He who made the eye shall He not see?" "Shall man be more just than his Maker?" "Do men gather grapes from a thorn or figs from a thistle," or good fruit from an evil tree? Man is the most perfect fruit of the world of our experience; and goodness is the highest output of man's best energies. If we read goodness or wisdom into anything outside ourselves, self is the key; we suppose that like actions in others have the same hidden spiritual motives as our own; our first spontaneous thought, corrected only later by reflection, conceives Nature as if it were the work of a fellow-man, and we ask: What sort of man is he? how wise? how good? how powerful? And at once we are confronted with a medley of good and evil, kindness and cruelty, understanding and blindness, strength and weakness. If he is wholly good and kind then he either cannot or does not know how to give effect to his kindness; if he knows how, he either lacks the means or the good-will; if he possesses the means he fails either in goodness or understanding. Moreover, since goodness, wisdom, and power are three names for the same simple perfection in God, if He is limited in one respect He is limited in all three.

Some have tried to show that goodness and kindness are the rule, and seeming cruelty the exception; that happiness so predominates over unhappiness as to make creation consistent with Divine benevolence. Even were this demonstrable (which may very well be questioned) within the narrow range of human experience, direct and indirect, how can we be justified in arguing from the nature of this its infinitesimal fraction to that of the whole universe? Can we possibly prove that there evil is not the rule and goodness the exception? Is it not more conceivable that an evil power should do ever so much good for evil ends, than that a good power should do ever so little evil that good may come? As the cat fondles and plays with her victim and lets it fancy itself free to escape, so perhaps Nature smiles on us and beguiles us with many liberties and pleasures only that she may kill us many times over before putting us out of pain.

Others say, truly enough, that the inability to realise absurdities or inherent impossibilities is no slur on omnipotence; and they suggest that, taking all the divine attributes into consideration, the existing amount of evil is the minimum necessary price of the existing amount of good. But it is a mere conjecture, and one which ill-consorts with that conception of Divine liberty which is needed for religious faith and hope. Moreover, the nature of things is founded in, and reflects the nature of God; if therefore in the very nature of things, and, if of absolute necessity, good can only be attained through so much evil, and joy through so much pain, can we say that the nature of things is obviously good and kind, and that it reveals to us the perfect goodness and kindness of its archetype, the divine nature?

Still feebler are the attempts to grapple

with the problem of sin and of the ruin of
souls; with the ravages wrought in man's
spirit by passion, temptation and ignorance
for which often neither he nor his parents are
responsible. We can fancy a wise and good
man's sometimes seeming (but only seeming)
callous and hard in regard to the bodily pain,
weariness, sorrows and afflictions of others,
on the grounds that he foresees certain moral
and spiritual advantages that will, or at least
ought, to result to the sufferer from the
enduring of these things. And so too, we
can conceive that in many cases at least
(though not in the case of very young
children, or of the insane or otherwise
irresponsible) God's goodness might force
Him to cause or permit those sufferings if
they were the absolutely necessary condition
of the moral growth of finite spirits. But on
the face of it the world seems to be arranged
with even more wholesale callous indifference
to moral ruin, than to physical and emotional
suffering—"Strait is the gate, and narrow
the way, and few there be that find it." We
would fain comfort ourselves by the hope
that in spite of invincible ignorance, invincible passion, invincible weakness, good-will

may have free-play in all alike, and that those who, according to our social and ethical standard, are the last may be the first before Him who knows all and allows for all, who looks to the will's bent and direction, rather than to its attainment. But even this hope falters when we remember that the will to attain righteousness demands a belief in the goodness and attainableness of the object— a belief that perishes through pressure of ignorance, bad example and temptation. Success in moral and religious attainment creates and increases the will to succeed; but in the measure that failure is seen to be inevitable, the will dwindles down to mere velleity, and finally to extinction.

XVIII.

BELIEF IN GOD'S GOODNESS AND WISDOM.

(2.)

THE attempts to make our belief in a God of infinite goodness, wisdom, and power, fit in harmoniously with our view of the world around us, as given us by experience and systematised by our understanding, are, and will always remain, inadequate. Faith alone is equal to the burden—the Faith that cries: " Though He should slay me yet will I trust in Him ;" not a blind witless faith, a hugging of comfortable illusions, a prophesying of smooth things and deceits; nor even a dutiful submission to a purely external revelation of dogmatic mysteries; but a preferential choice of the instinctive dictates of our religious sense as against the more fallible inferences of our understanding drawn from infinitely limited data.

Not that Faith contradicts, but that it supplements those data, or rather believes firmly in the existence of some as yet unknown and unknowable supplement and complement by which God shall "save His word in all things and yet make all well which is not well." For at least we can conceive that sorrow *may* be joy in the making—not merely a stepping-stone to joy, something to be left behind and forgotten; but a constituent element of joy, something to be perpetuated and remembered. For, life as we know it, whether of the body or of the mind or of the will, means action; and action means the overcoming of what is counter to our will,—of what, as such, fulfils the very definition of evil; so that, as we know them, good and evil are inseparable correlatives.

Christianity has consecrated this Faith, symbolised in the Cross, that sorrow shall not merely give place to, but shall be turned into joy, shall furnish the very stuff and texture on which joy is to be embroidered. And this aid was well-timed; for just in the measure that this faith in God's goodness becomes an imperative spiritual exigency, it becomes more intellectually difficult. When divinity was partitioned among a multitude of holders it was not hard to credit any one of them with perfect goodness and to ascribe all evil to his rival deities; nor was it difficult when the one God was viewed as in conflict with eternal matter, or with some necessary principle of evil. But the more purely he was conceived as the Alpha and Omega of all things, so much the more pressing became the problem of that evil for which He and He alone was felt to be ultimately responsible, whether as doer or as permitter.

Yet however great an advance this purer monotheism may be upon less worthy notions of divinity it does not, and perhaps cannot, wholly deliver us from the need of conceiving God man-wise, and from judging His departures from our standard of goodness as due to defect rather than to excess. It is as when a selfish and ungenerous man who can understand no higher motive than self-interest sees nothing in another's self-sacrifice but a failure of prudence; nor can he realize any sense in which even prudence itself might dictate this apparent failure of prudence. What *faute de mieux* we call "goodness" in God, but what were better called God-ness, may infinitely transcend our goodness, and yet for this very reason produce seemingly contrary effects.

Again, when we rightly revolt against deism in favour of a truer conception of God as being also immanent in creation, we are apt to think of Him too pantheistically as a sort of world-soul whose character is revealed in the form and movement of creation just as that of our own soul is revealed through our body. And this we imply when we criticise Nature as kind or cruel, wise or foolish, good or evil, as though we were dealing with a person; or when we fancy that we have an immediate revelation of the Divine character in Nature—a fancy which is at the root of a good deal of the cheaper sort of blasphemy. This may be no better than arguing from the accuracy of a watch to the punctuality of the watchmaker, or than assuming that a portrait must resemble the portrait-painter. Only as indicating the end and purpose of its author and his skill in attaining it does his production throw light on his character and nature.

If Nature be but a mechanism or "determinism," we are as wrong in calling it kind or wise, as in calling it cruel or unwise; it can have no more moral character than a windmill except so far as it is personified. The only pertinent question would be: What purpose does it indicate in its author, and how far does it fulfil that purpose? To answer this would demand an almost infinite comprehensiveness of experience and perspicacity of judgment.

Yet this mechanical or determinist view of the world is just the one which harmonises best with the exigencies of the higher spiritual life, and which is thereby proved to possess an analogous representative value. Accurate it cannot be, yet it may be the nearest approach to accuracy of which we are capable.

Only so far as the world is law-bound and regular, and as we understand its laws and regularities, we are able to deal with it at all. Our subjective or spiritual growth consists in extending our mastery over the world, in comprehending it and subjecting it to our action. Law is thus the presupposition of life and of the development of our personality; in a world governed wholly by caprice or in which endless and incalculable relaxations of law were tolerated we should remain children for ever. By opposing and overcoming the world through our understanding of it, our freedom is expanded and strengthened and all things are put under our feet. As the opposite and counterpart of our will and freedom, this vast determinism is the great all-inclusive Evil which is the very condition of our goodness ; it is the foe whose conquest is our glory; whose persistent opposition calls forth those undeveloped and unguessed spiritual energies by which it is over-matched and robbed of its sting while retaining its strength and utility. By eliciting the deepest protest of our soul— the protest of sentiment, and of utterance, and of active opposition—the bewilderments, the scandals, the godlessness of the world bring out and stablish all that is best in us, and range us on God's side against all that is opposed to the Divine Will as revealed in the best aspirations of our own. Partial truth is a lie when it is taken for the whole ; viewed as an adequate image of God, needing no explanatory complement, this infinitesimal fraction of reality which we call the world were rather a blasphemous idol, a libel on the divine Wisdom and Goodness, the very embodiment of Evil and Folly. For evil is the caricature or parody of goodness: and folly, that of wisdom. Because an automaton may be made to look and to act in some way like a man, its unlikenesses are all the more ludicrous. The law-bound mechanism of the world must necessarily simulate in many of its effects the infinite wisdom and goodness of its Author; but it works blindly and blunderingly as a mill, and betrays at every turn its lack of inherent consciousness and intention. Viewed, as we must view it, out of its explanatory context, the world must seem bad, and is bad so far as it is opposed to the Divine Will as expressed in our highest ideals; and yet this badness is even already revealed to us as constitutive of goodness on a higher plane; for to refuse the world, to oppose it, to correct it, to overcome it, is the labour by which our mind and will are brought into conformity with the Divine. And in this labour we feel ourselves fellow-workers and free instruments of that indwelling God whom, knowing to be infinite, we must think of as equivalently finite and as the eternal ideal of perfected humanity; as one afflicted in all our afflictions; as sharing our griefs and carrying our sorrows; as crucified with us on the cross of this ruthless determinism which His own hands have prepared to be the instrument of our deliverance and deification, and on which He Himself is racked and tormented, in us and with us.

XIX.

BELIEF IN GOD AS CREATOR.

In the light of much that has already been said, the belief in God's universal Creatorship scarcely needs separate treatment. It is as to the ultimate author of his being, or at least as to the highest controller of his destiny that man first turns to God in religious worship. The sense that he has not made himself, that he his not his own, that his fate in life and death is not at his own command, the vague sense of absolute dependence on unknown power and will, lead him more simply and instinctively to some notion of an author and maker of the world than could any clear and conscious reasoning from effects to causes. Naturally God is first conceived as working like ourselves, as shaping some given matter according to a certain pattern or idea, as moulding man from the earth to His own semblance, and breathing into his nostrils the breath of His own nostrils. It is in point of immeasurable complexity and of infinite power and skill that His workmanship is conceived to differ from our own, rather than in kind. Generation being with us an unintelligent mode of production of which even plant-life is capable and in which we are more passive than active, is a less suitable category than that of manufacture whereby to explain the Divine productivity which we feel must be conscious and intentional.

God, as soon as He is viewed as more than the ancestor of a tribe or race, is called the Maker rather than the Generator of the world and of man. Yet later reflection on religious experience gropes after some blending of the excellencies of makership and fatherhood — of the transcendency of the artist in regard to his fabrication, and of the community of nature between parent and offspring. With a growing appreciation of the Divine unity, the Maker and Manager of all things in heaven and earth is felt to be something infinitely more and other than a maker; His causality, like His Being with which it is identical, is felt to be of a wholly different order to aught within our experience. Yet higher than our own will and its spiritual control of our bodily frame we cannot rise in imagination. At best we can think of God as bringing all things into being by a similar act of will: "He spake and they were made; He commanded and they were created." But even this more spiritualised notion of divine causality is in terms of the human and finite and is a combination of irreconcilable notions. For will, in the only form in which we can conceive it, can move and alter and overcome the "given," but cannot produce it: it can originate movement but not substance. In giving the name of "will" to that which is the origin of our own will we are ascribing to the cause the name and nature of its effect. To "create," *i.e.* "make out of nothing," explains the mystery of Divine Causality and of God's relation to His creatures, as combining in some higher but unknown unity the excellencies of two irreconcilable conceptions. God is the Maker in point of conscious skill and intelligence in production; He is the Father and Begetter in point of the vitality and naturalness of the mode of production and of the relation of closeness and affection and loving care founded upon His fatherhood; but the infinite "Other" in which all this is merged and transformed evades all possibility of understanding; we can no more define "creation" than we can define God. We face the idea as a dumb animal might face a printed page or some other product of intelligence; all that it sees is there, but how much more than it sees! We however must and do believe in that incomprehensible surplus that lies beyond the limits of our comprehension and which holds the answer to our riddles—riddles that are inseparable from our necessity of thinking of God as making, designing, begetting, managing, contriving, after the image and likeness of man.

The process by which the idea of God's causality has been purified from one limitation after another, has been enriched with the perfection of every known kind of authorship and origination, and has been extended to the whole realm of finite existence and movement, bodily and spiritual, is due chiefly to the development of the religious sense and to the expanding exigencies of the spiritual life. Its trueness to the ultimate nature of things is established by the test of life; for though the belief is not universal, it is universally life-giving and liberating. The soul needs for its fulness of life that sense which can only be called a sense of "creatureship" of most intimate dependence on One who is "dearer than father, mother, child or spouse;" "closer than breathing, nearer than hands or feet"—the soul's own soul, as it were; one "in whom we live and move and are," not as a part lives and moves in the organism to which it belongs at the cost of its own freedom and individuality, but with an infinitely closer intimacy that yet saves our freedom and separateness; one to whom we are bound, not as word is bound to word in speech, but rather somewhat as the spoken word is bound to the thought which it incorporates, by which it is enveloped and permeated, and from which it can be severed only by some witless ear sensitive to the sound but dead to the sense.

But the difficulties and perplexities so freely suggested by this human conception of God as a spirit within our spirit, a mind within our mind, a will within our will, would quickly imperil that conception and rob us of its practical fruitfulness did we not pass on to the explicit recognition of its tentative and analogous character; and thus a somewhat philosophic notion of "creation" as distinct from even the most idealised makership or fatherhood, has become an exigency of the fuller spiritual life.

The division of the realm of creation into heaven and earth may have been originally directed against the belief that ascribed divinity and the control of man's fate to the visible heavens, the sun, moon, and stars; but later reflection explained it as equivalent to the distinction between invisible and visible, spiritual and material, as given us in the prayer "Our Father who art in Heaven, Thy will be done on earth as it is in Heaven." The "invisible" is not here co-extensive with the world of reality as opposed to the world of appearances, for the former embraces the infinite and uncreated as well as the created. But that dualism which is forced upon us by the highest development of religious and moral life as being at least fundamentally and equivalently true, tends to resolve creation into the opposed and complementary realms of freedom and determinism, of subject and object, the one (according to fruitful conceit of the schoolmen) being the *imago* or semblance, the other the *vestigium*, the footprint or trace of the Creator.

For indeed considered in false abstraction, and apart from its relation to the spiritual and moral life of the subject, the world is stamped with no more than a footprint of the Divinity—with a sign that He was once there and has passed by; it shows a limited and unconscious intelligence and purpose such as a mechanism might owe to the past creative act of its contriver. Its goodness and wisdom are but caricatures of the divine, blasphemous because of their very traces of likeness; mimicking the Creator as a marionette mimics its living maker. Nor must we be deceived by the vast scale on which those traces are manifested; for if there are signs of an intelligence and benevolence beyond all possible measure of human capacity, these are more than cancelled by the scale on which failure in both respects is apparent. If no man could be so good or wise as Nature seems, neither could any man be so cruel or wanton. Only in the goodness of character have we anything that may reverently be called an "image" of the indwelling Goodness of God: only as considered in its essential relation to freedom and character is the realm of determinism redeemed from badness, and a basis found for the faith that the world's seeming failures have their explanation in him to whom the difference of Subject and Object, of Freedom and Determinism, is at once saved and overcome.

The conception of Nature as being, apart from man, a direct expression or self-manifestation of the Divine character is responsible for the moral and spiritual perversions that are everywhere associated with polytheistic or pantheistic Nature-worship. To worship the caricature of divinity there revealed to us is really to worship the Devil transformed into an angel of light, for truth out of its context is the worst of lies; and good arrested in the making may be the deadliest of evils.

XX.

BELIEF IN THE INCARNATION.

(1.)

APOTHEOSIS, the deification of heroes, is a frequent manifestation of the natural idolatry of the human mind. A low conception of the meaning of divinity, the fanatical exaggerations of hero-worship, the fertility of the myth-making faculty, the craving for a god in our own image and likeness, combine with other causes to make the error easy and almost inevitable. Nor are incarnation-beliefs less easy of explanation where gods, conceived more or less in the form and fashion of men, may well be imagined as mixing with mortals and even marrying into the race. In such superstitions or diseases of the religious sense, we must not let the perversion blind us to the value of that which is perverted, or overlook the natural exigency or appetite that gropes blindly for satisfaction in these husks of truth. Rather we must recognise in them bizarre "dreamings of things to come," troubling "the prophetic soul of the wide world;" uncouth embryo shapes of the fuller faith that is ours, vain essays of inexperienced humanity to interpret its own nature and needs. We must moreover distinguish the principle of variation from the principle of selection; the various fallacies, truths, half-truths, and errors, the good, the evil and the mixed motives, that have first almost accidentally suggested and shaped these beliefs, from that practically proven religious value that has determined their survival. The desire to bring the human and divine, this world and the other, into closer relation; to rend the dividing veil of the heavens; to lift man up to the throne of the immortal gods: to draw the gods down to the sorrows and weaknesses of man's mortal lot has rarely dictated and originated, but it has mostly sustained and won credit for beliefs of this kind—beliefs which, so far, may have served, in default of better, as a rude language or channel of communication between men and that Unknown God whose goodness they ignorantly worshipped under the image and likeness of some creature of their brain.

Yet, as in other instances, it was needful that the little seed of truth should perish in order to live again in a higher form; that a purer and better conception of the divine nature should first put such a gulf between Creator and creature as to make apotheoses and incarnations unthinkable and blasphemous, and that a clearer apprehension of the infinitude of God's greatness should prepare the way for a belief in the infinitude of His mercy and condescension, and in the mystery of the Son of God made man to make men sons of God.

Thus while Christianity with its Trinity of Divine persons, its God-made-man, its pantheon of divinised men and women, is open to the superficial charge of being a falling-away from the purer monotheism of Jew or Mahometan, and a reversion to the old pagan polytheistic type, it is rather to be regarded as taking up into a higher synthesis those advantages of polytheism which had to be sacrificed for the greater advantages of a too abstract and soul-starving monotheism. For as has already been said, the unsocial conception of the divinity as a solitary infinite spirit, out of all fatherly and friendly relationship with the finite, is as untrue for deeper philosophical reflection as it is for the best instincts of the spiritual life. Nor has Judaism been really content with it; God as the God of Israel, as the God of the individual soul, as the Father of the human race is already limited and incarnate for the mind that so regards Him; He is virtually a " God with us."

The belief in the Godhead of Christ is the capital and central creation of the spirit of Christ. A mystery for metaphysics, its meaning as a practical rule of speech, sentiment and conduct is within the apprehension of the simplest follower of the Galilean fisherman who first accepted it. For to believe a truth is to reckon with it as with a reality, whether welcome or unwelcome; it is to adapt our will to it as to a new factor of the world with which we have to deal. Here it means to speak of Christ, to feel and to act towards Him as towards a person who, being one and the same, possesses distinctly all the attributes of divinity and of humanity; it means for us that the life and death of

Christ are the life and death, not of the divinest of men or of the greatest of prophets, but of God. What saint or prophet could dare to say, "Take and eat; this is My body"? Who but God is the bread of the soul's life?

Christocentricism, the direct adoration of Christ as personally identical with God, is the essential characteristic of Christian as distinct from any purely theistic religious sentiment. The Catholic doctrine is far less a creation of theological reflection than of the selective power of the Christian spirit rejecting the variations of heretical curiosity—Arian, Nestorian, Monophysite—as inadequate to its needs, as untrue to the laws of its life. It is a synthesis of all their religious values and a correction of all their deficiencies. No incarnate aeon, no created Wisdom or Logos could bridge the gulf between the finite creature and the infinite Creator; no alliance with a servant could win us the adoption of sons. The chiefest of His angels are but ministering spirits; and those nearest His throne are not, as measured by infinity, appreciably nearer than we are. It is Himself we need to see and handle and no angel from His face. Nor yet are the higher exigencies of religion satisfied by any sort of Nestorian Christology. Between person and person the separateness is irreducible; no relation of closeness that leaves this opposition unconquered or that falls short of that of personal identity between the God-Christ and the Man-Christ can lend the same emotional and practical value to the life at Nazareth and the death on Calvary. Saint of Saints, Prince of Prophets and Martyrs, First-born of every creature, the Man-Christ were at best a divinely-given ideal of perfect humanity—God's shadow but not His substance and very self.

If in revolt against this merely moral or juridical union of the human and divine in Christ the Monophysite secures unity of person at the cost of blending or confusion of the two natures into something that is neither one nor the other, he seems to relapse from pure monotheism into an essentially pagan mode of thought inconsistent with a right estimate of the unchangeableness and infinitude of the Godhead. Still more, he robs the Incarnation of its principal religious value; for it is as being both perfect God and perfect man, as leading two different lives at once, that Christ fulfils the ideal of a mediator. For this reason the instinct of the Christian spirit has ever been hostile to any sort of Docetanism that would deliver Christ from any of the blameless and natural limitations of our human nature, and so make Him less of a mediator touched with a feeling for our infirmities, tempted in all points as we, yet never yielding to sin. It is the faith that God not only knows this sad life of ours but that He has actually lived it and consecrated it, which has transformed the bitter water of our affliction into the wine of joy and gladness. It is therefore Christian devotion rather than Christian metaphysics, the need of the soul rather than the need of the intellect, that has selected the orthodox faith in preference to heterodox error.

XXI.

BELIEF IN THE INCARNATION.

(2.)

THAT God, in His own simple and mysterious perfection, realises, while He infinitely transcends, the highest idealisation of human excellence ; that so far He is man, and that in striving after the ideal completion of our nature we are likening ourselves to God, making ourselves His sons ; that since our spiritual life requires we should conceive Him in our own finite likeness (as another, though indefinitely greater, personal spirit in relation with our own, endowed with like faculties working under like conditions), this conception must have some equivalent representative value—all this seems more than probable to that deeper theistic philosophy which reckons with the whole man, and not merely with the rational understanding.

By its doctrine of the Incarnation the

Christian spirit expresses this truth in the language of fact, and brings it home effectually to the imagination and emotion of the flesh-clad spirit of man. The aforesaid ideal of the Perfect Man which is swallowed up and transcended in the infinitude and simplicity of the Divine Perfection is, as it were, hewn out of that eternal rock and set in all the beauty and definiteness of its outline before us for our eyes to see and our hands to handle, being yet bound to God by the tie of personal unity and not severed after the manner of other creatures. In Christ that aspect of the Godhead which is the highest our human standards can measure, and under which God is the postulate of our moral and religious life, is thrown into bright relief against what to us is the inscrutable darkness, but is really the blinding brilliance, of that absolute perfection which embraces but infinitely transcends it:

> So the All-Great were the All-Loving too,
> So through the thunder comes a human voice
> Saying: O heart I made, a heart beats here,
> Face, my hands fashioned, see it in myself.

"He that has seen Me hath seen the Father; how sayest thou then: 'Show us the Father?'" Christ is the most perfect translation of the Divine Nature and Character into terms of human nature and character; whatever there is in Him of truth and grace, of wisdom and mercy, of strength and love, all that and infinitely more is contained in the simplicity of the Divine Perfection which it is His mission to unfold to us. The Catholic and Christian spirit has refused to regard Him as mediating between an angered Master and His rebel servants, as commissioned by these latter to overcome the reluctance of the former. God so loved the world that He gave His only-begotten Son, that He "sent Him into the world" as ambassador to plead the Father's cause with His erring children; to win them to a belief in His loving-kindness—a belief which was hard for them so long as, being themselves merciless and unforgiving, they were bound to conceive Him in their own image and likeness. Nothing could be more unlike the various pagan and superstitious notions of mediation and atonement.

Christ is thus the incarnation of the eternal humanity, *i.e.* of humanity as it is involved and merged in the simplicity of the

Divine Perfection and identified with God. But humanity stands here for the manhood of an unit, not for the whole race of Adam as bound together physically, spiritually, and morally into one living social organism. Through Christ whose human nature is knit and woven into the continuity of its substance this collective humanity is indirectly linked to the Godhead and thereby to its own eternal ideal. Through Christ in whose manhood the ideal manhood is realised, grace is spread abroad among men in order slowly to realise the ideal race, people, or kingdom of God. Through Him who is a Son of God by Nature in virtue of His personality, all men can receive power to become sons of God by adoption fashioned to the pattern of Christ's human spirit and character. For the infinite riches and potentiality of the Spirit of Christ could not find adequate expression within the compass of any single mortal life however full and varied, but needs to be manifested in every variety of time and place, character and circumstances; in its social no less than in its individual effects; in combination with strength and weakness, wisdom and simplicity, culture and barbarism, riches and poverty, age and youth, antiquity and modernity.

Brought to the test of life, how does this doctrine compare with pagan beliefs in apotheoses and incarnations springing from and fostering unworthy views of the dignity of God and man? Surely the truth of Christ's humanity, taken in connection with that of His divinity, is one that has, more than all others, renewed the face of the earth. It has turned a feeble and ineffectual speculation of philosophy into a living effectual truth of religion: it has brought home to the heart of mankind the infinite value of the individual soul, the ineffaceable dignity of personality; it is a belief to which we owe that slow movement of liberation, which is lifting our race from conditions of brute competition to that of free children in the same household; a belief through which the old scholastic speculation about the angels, affirming that each was a species in itself and could not, without contradiction, be repeated or multiplied, has come to be verified of man viewed on his spiritual side. Jesus, the Son of God by nature, and every man the brother of Christ by nature and adoption—is a belief which gives us an insight into the world of wills and explains a thousand mysterious instincts of unity and sameness, which else we should never have been able to formulate. The oneness of all men with one another in Christ; and their oneness with God through Christ, is the foundation of all practical and affective religion as summed up in the duty of Charity; and this is the religious value of our belief in "Jesus Christ—His only Son—our Lord." All that is added in the Nicene and Athanasian creeds as to the precise nature of the hypostatic union— "Begotten of the Father before all worlds: not made; consubstantial with the Father; by whom all things were made," and so forth; all this is but protective of the simple truth that Christ is God; and that God is in Christ, reconciling the world to Himself.

Again, the doctrine of the Incarnation which is given us by the spirit of Christianity and which is the intellectual expression of the implications of the Christian sentiment of divine love, is also the supreme consecration of that sacramental principle which is so potent a factor in the development of spiritual life. The precise relation of reality to appearance, of inward to outward, of the spirit to the flesh, of active freedom to passive necessity, of the determining to the determined, is one of the persistent problems of the soul the solution of which seems to evade that rational understanding whose forms are derived from, and whose language is adapted to, the lower member only of each antithesis ; and which can figure the relation of its own sphere to the higher only in terms of those relations that obtain between the contents of the lower. Only by giving the soul certain attributes of the body can it figure to itself some analogy of the tie between body and soul.

The sacramental principle, as demanded by the exigencies of Christian sanctity, gives us at least a practical answer whose proven fidelity to the laws of life warrants our faith in its fundamental truthfulness. A neo-platonic or puritanical abhorrence of the sense-world as radically and irredeemably evil and hostile to the spiritual life marks the first crude revolt against mere pagan Naturalism or against the abuse and corruption of the sacramental principle. A partial correction of this extreme is found in the " sacramentarian" view of Nature as a symbolic expression or sign of the spiritual order, as of something separate and distinct, with which it has no causal connection except so far as by enlightening man's intelligence it may occasion some movement of his will and affections. And this is analogous to Nestorianism in Christology; and receives a sort of Monophysite correction in the view that conceives the relationship between Nature and Spirit, Outward and Inward, after the fashion of a material mixture or confusion of substance. All these errors have been excluded by the *Lex Orandi*, by the instinct of the Christian spirit, which teaches us that Nature is the instrument of our healing as of our hurt: " Peccat caro; mundat caro." Unconquered and blindly obeyed Nature stands as an impenetrable barrier between man and God; conquered and brought under the will it becomes the organ of the divinity, the channel of communication between spirit and spirit;—not merely symbolising but effecting what it symbolises. Thus the sacred humanity of Christ is the sacrament of sacraments; for there the subjugation of the natural to the spiritual is absolute as in no other; His manhood is no mere finite symbol of the divinity, but is divine; not mingled nor confounded with divinity, but united to it personally: Christ is for us effectually that which He reveals and signifies. In Him the redemption of Nature, the conversion of evil into good, of poison into medicine, reaches its unique culmination; through Him and in union with Him the visible order becomes the sacrament, the effective symbol, of the invisible.

But while this relationship between the godhead and manhood of Christ is intelligible in terms of its practical consequences for us, in itself it cannot be represented to our mind except by halting analogies. If we are so vague as to the precise meaning of human personality; as to the relation of body and soul; and still more as to the relation of creature to Creator; we are not likely to form any very coherent representation of the "Hypostatic Union." At best it is a name for that hidden mystery in which the practical truth of our conceptions of Christ is founded.

We may illustrate it from psychology

which gives us cases of so-called divided personality, but which are rather cases of double nature in the same personality—cases where two complete and separate systems of knitted memories, ideas, feelings, habits, passions, are developed in the same person who may be, but often is not aware of this doubleness of nature, mind and will. Or, with the Athanasian Creed, we may illustrate it from the normal union of soul and body— of two substances in one person. Or we may illustrate it from the ethical side of personality as an absolute and unique subjection of the created will to the divine, destroying every vestige of "otherness" and passing beyond all other finite sanctity, *in aliud genus*, making the sacred humanity not merely a separable instrument but a living inseparable organ of the Divine will. Taken as defective metaphors these comparisons are helpful; taken as more than this, they are false and misleading. What they point to lies beyond the range of our mental vision for ever, since it demands a comprehension of the Infinite.

XXII.

BELIEF IN FACTS OF RELIGIOUS HISTORY.

CHRISTIANITY is an historical religion ; that is to say, it proposes certain historical facts, no less than theoretical statements, for our belief; and as these latter have to be reconciled with the philosophy of our understanding—with our world-theory, so the former have to be reconciled with our reading of history. Jesus Christ is not a purely ideal creation like King Arthur, but an historical personage ; He has a place, not only in the world of thought, but also in the world of fact. Our construction of either world must find room for Him. In and through Him the ideal has been realised, the Word has been made flesh and has dwelt among us.

As a mere dream of the religious sense

the Gospel might have been a divinely inspired work of great spiritual fruitfulness, like the *Divina Commedia* or the *Pilgrim's Progress;* it might have conveyed a true God-given revelation of the absolute order in the clothing of analogy; it might have possessed a regulative and practical truth as a guide to life, as a way of taking things. Many who hold it to be no more than a dream, freely admit that it has been thus beneficent; but they must also allow that it has been beneficent to a great extent just because it was held to be solid fact and not simple dream-stuff.

Between the inward and the outward, between the world of reality and the world of appearances, the relation is not merely one of symbolic correspondence. The distinction that is demanded by the dualism of our mind does not exclude, but implies and presupposes, a causal and dynamic unity of the two. Our view of the value of the outward world should be "sacramental" rather than "sacramentarian," that is, we should look upon it as being an effectual symbol of the inward, in consequence of its natural and causal connection therewith; and not merely as signifying truths to our intelligence, which can become effectual only through the subsequent action of our will.

If certain beliefs are universally fruitful of spiritual progress it is, as we have said, because they are rooted in fact, and possess at least an analogous representative value; it is because through them we are put into relation with reality. And this relation is one of action and reaction; of giving and taking, taking and giving. The beliefs are not arbitrary, like algebraic symbols, but are, like our sense-perceptions, the natural response of our mind to the influence of its surroundings. We are passive before we are active; we receive impressions before we attempt to imagine their causes and laws; or to govern our action in the light of such imaginings. Thus by experience we feel our way to more and more adequate conceptions of the world we live in. It is because God's influence in us or upon us is from the first that of a father, that we at last come to believe in His fatherhood; but the belief makes Him more effectually a father than ever; just as every truer hypothesis about Nature multiplies our communication with

Nature and leads to fuller knowledge and power.

Hence the belief is sacramental; it not merely signifies the relation of which it is the natural issue or evidence, but it also effects and deepens that relation. There can therefore be no ultimate conflict between what is true for the religious life and what is true for the understanding—philosophical or historical. In the measure that a creed has regulative and practical truth, it is also representative, however mysteriously, of the same world which our understanding strives to reconstruct from the data and in terms of outward experience. That the two reconstructions, using different and partial data and proceeding by such diverse methods, should often disagree both negatively and positively, is only natural. The criterion of faith (taken widely) is simply the practical one of proved universal religious value, "Quod semper," &c. The believer is justified in showing that philosophical and historical reasoning tallies with, or does not contradict his belief, but in this he plays the rôle not of believer but of philosopher or historian. Further, in case of conflict, he is justified in preferring to hold on to an otherwise rationally indefensible belief until its religious value is accounted for and saved in some higher truth.

Thus a Unitarian might deny the Trinity until he were persuaded that the Unity of God was saved and transcended in that doctrine; or the Incarnation, until he were convinced that it was compatible with the Divine immutability. Faith will never allow him to deny a belief of proved religious value.

As our philosophy is a putting-together of all experience, past as well as present, with a view to understanding this world as it is, and dealing with it rightly, so too our creed is based largely on the data of history, on what has happened to us personally, and to our race from the beginning, in regard to our spiritual life and our dealings with God. There more especially, though also in every other section of experience, the Ideal has been slowly realising itself, the Word has been embodying itself. Religion is not a dream, but an enacted, self-expression of the spiritual world—a parable uttered, however haltingly, in the language of fact.

It is not an arbitrary working hypothesis shaped at one stroke by some comprehensive genius, but a construction that has been forced upon us and verified by our experience, step by step, and part by part. Hence it is, that certain concrete historical facts enter into our creed as matters of faith. Precisely as historical facts they concern the historian and must be criticised by his methods. But as matters of faith they must be determined by the criterion of faith, *i.e.* by their proved religious values as universally effectual of spiritual progress; as implications of the spirit of Christian charity and sanctity; as selected by the exigencies of the development of the inner life of the soul. The unity of all experience forbids any ultimate contradiction between the results of these separate criteria; but it does not exclude the possibility of superficial and temporary contradictions. The believer will desire and endeavour to play the part of historian and to harmonise every seeming discord, often with more zeal than discretion or ingenuousness. But he will always be justified in holding to the faith-taught facts until he is convinced that their religious value is in no way imperilled by the results of historical criticism.

Our reading of history is in some sort a "perception;" that is to say, from certain points, hints and suggestions which are all that is really given us, we construct what we call an "object," but what is more truly a "pro-ject," inasmuch as nine-tenths of what we imagine ourselves to see is thrown out into the object by our own fancies, memories, expectations, inferences, associations—just as in a dim light we shape every shadow according to our fears. Taken as a whole, the Christian reading of history, the religious interpretation of the aforesaid points, hints and suggestions will frequently differ from the readings inspired by other and counter interests. In many matters it has had to yield to historical criticism and may yet have to yield; but of its substantial justness faith can have no doubt; nor can it have any doubt even as to details which are essentially bound up with any indispensable religious value. Such facts however faith holds by their religious, not by their historical, side. To believe that Christ was crucified under Pontius Pilate, or even that He rose from the dead and ascended into Heaven, may need as little faith as to believe that Wellington won the battle of Waterloo. Faith holds to these facts as fruitful of eternal life, and on purely conscientious and religious grounds ; *Lex orandi, lex credendi*—the rule of prayer is the rule of belief.

XXIII.

THE PRAYER-VALUE OF OTHER BELIEFS.

(1.)

WHEN we turn to the historical statements about our Lord—"born of the Virgin Mary, suffered under Pontius Pilate, was crucified, dead and buried," &c., we have therefore to distinguish between the historical and religious value, and to remember that it is only for the sake of the latter that the Church interests herself in the former. What then is the religious value of the fact that Christ was miraculously conceived and born of a virgin? Theologically it has no essential connection with the Incarnation. The God-man might have been naturally conceived and born, and a sinner might have been conceived and born miraculously. According to popular ideas, partly derived from pagan sources, to have been born of a virgin miraculously through the intervention of a divine person, would have enhanced the dignity of Christ; but the puerility of such a claim would have been quite out of keeping with the sober spirituality of the Gospel. We have little hesitation in sweeping aside nine-tenths of the marvels recorded in the apocryphal gospels; not precisely because they are marvels, but because they lack all religious significance and show themselves to be the fruit of a mere wonder-lust, and not inspirations of the religious spirit. They were created by the mouth-to-mouth gossip of that multitude of nominal Christians, to whom Christ was only a greater than Solomon, or than Simon Magus, and in whose hearts the spirituality of the Gospel and its protest against religious materialism found no echo.

True, it must be allowed that the esteem of mere physiological (as distinct from spiritual) virginity, which prevailed far on into Christian times, had no better origin than in Oriental superstition. To some extent it is also traceable to that dualistic asceticism of which Plato is the most cultivated exponent, and which influenced the mind of St. Augustine so profoundly. Where monogamy prevails the sexual impulse is so often more or less illicit and hostile to monogamy that it is hard to dissociate even its lawful indulgence from some taint of sinfulness. As a feat of self-restraint in the interests of duty, an inviolate chastity has an undoubted moral worth that is not unnaturally attached by association to the physiological conditions of such inviolacy. It is in these directions that we are to look for the explanation of the popular estimate of bodily virginity —not unallied to the reverence given to pillar-saints and prodigies of fasting and other austerities. The animal-minded multitude is as much impressed and astonished by the conquest of animalism as by any miracle, and cares more about the marvel, than about the motive (moral or non-moral) of which it is but the contingent expression.

It is not in deference to such modes of thought that Christianity affirms the virginity of Mary as honourable to the Mother and to her Son; still less as wishing to explain the Incarnation in pagan fashion as the result of commerce between a divinity and a woman. If we would find the religious and spiritual value of the doctrine we must seek it in the influence it has in fact exercised upon the heart of Christians and Saints. We must see in the Virgin Mother the highest expression and embodiment of Christian sanctity which the Holy Spirit has brought forth in the hearts of the faithful; and, in the last resort, we must see in her the revelation of a new aspect of the Divine Goodness with which we are thus put into fuller and more fruitful communication. Who can deny that the Christian spirit has been fed and fostered by this belief as much as by that of the Passion, or the Incarnation, or the Eucharistic Presence? Yet, plainly, it is not the flesh but the spirit that quickeneth; it is not the physical facts that matter, but the religious values which they symbolise. That the sanctity and sinlessness of Mary, as Christ's mother, is the sole religious significance of her virginity, will be questioned by no one. "Blessed is the womb that bore Thee!" expresses a lower conception of supernatural dignity than the amendment: "Yea, rather, Blessed are they that hear the word of God and keep it." As Christ opposes spiritual maternity to bodily; so also spiritual to bodily virginity. "He that doeth the will of my Father, the same is my brother and my sister and my mother," and of such spiritual nearness and kinship Mary stands as a sort of divinely constituted archetype in the Church of Christ. As in other matters (*e.g.*, in His Transfiguration and Ascension) so, too, in this, the spiritual truth is given to us not in the language of parable but in that of historical fact, which as such is subject to the criteria of history, though as the vehicle of a religious value, as the earthen vessel of a heavenly treasure, it is subject only to the criterion of faith.

As regards the other circumstances connected with the birth of Christ, a like discrimination between religious and historical values is not difficult. Thus as to the appearance of the Angels to the Shepherds. When we remember that according to theology an angel is an invisible and incorporeal being, it is manifest we are dealing with some kind of divine accommodation to human ways of thought. Subjective or objective, produced by the brain of the beholder or by something outside the brain, such an appearance of a human form where none exists is an illusion. At best, it is a visionary expression of an internal spiritual event. That God reveals Himself by preference to the simple; that the glory of God and the redemption of man is the meaning of Christ's earthly mission; that the Messiah was to be sought, not as worldly materialism had hoped, in the palaces of the great, but wrapt in swaddling clothes and laid in a manger—all this constitutes the religious value, the faith-matter, underlying the inspired narrative of the Evangelist. Were it merely a legend inspired, or selected and shaped, by some prophet full of the spirit of Christ, this religious value would not be affected; the only difference would be in the mode of expression—the difference between the language of facts and that of words and images; between an enacted and a spoken allegory.

Of these and other historical beliefs the whole religious value lies in the deeper and wider appreciation they give us of Christ's principles and aims and methods by showing us new applications of His spirit to new conditions. What He would have done (could we know it by revelation) were as instructive for us as what He actually did.

In some measure, His Saints, so far as they are filled with His spirit, extend His life in this way. In them we see Christ in other ages and conditions than those of His mortal life and learn more about Him. Similarly the Evangelists, full of His spirit and mind, might conceivably have been inspired to reveal Him to us, not in a strictly historical narrative, but in such fact-founded fictions as would best characterise and portray His personality to those who knew it not. Such literary devices were in no wise disreputable at a time when they were recognised and expected. Yet the difference between the pseudo-gospels and the inspired gospels would have remained infinite; the latter being truly divine revelations inspired by the spirit and mind of Christ, and that enthusiastic and appreciative love of Him, of which the writer was full—a love that instinctively idealised its object and clothed it in a garb best fitted to kindle a like love in other hearts; the former being the work of men untouched by the genuine spirit of Christ, who saw in Him naught but a magician or a sage, and who laboured to satisfy vulgar curiosity with a collection of mythical marvels void of all spiritual and religious significance.

If then these things do, as a fact, belong to history; if the lessons of the conception and birth of Christ have, as a fact, been embodied in actual events of the phenomenal world, and not merely in sacred or inspired legends, it is nevertheless important not to confound the historical with the religious value of such beliefs or to subject our faith to the perturbations and obscurities which may, from time to time, trouble the field of natural vision.

XXIV.

THE PRAYER-VALUE OF OTHER BELIEFS.

(2.)

We may pass over the articles which refer to the Passion and Death of Christ; first, because these events being in no wise miraculous have never been contested; and secondly, because their purely religious value is so obvious. Indeed it is the latter alone that makes them in any sense articles of faith, since the veriest infidel will not deny the historical facts. And this should make it clear that throughout it is in the internal and religious aspect of each article, not in the external and philosophical or historical, that faith finds its matter.

The descent into hell, or into the *Limbus Patrum* is, in its external aspect, to some extent an accommodation to current conceptions of the other world, as the very word "descended" shows. The religious value is found in the idea that Christ is the redeemer of all men from the beginning to the end; one whose day even Abraham rejoiced to see; that he is the realisation of the dreams of the old-world seers and prophets. Whatever sanctity has been attained in any age or race has been a participation of the sanctity of Christ, and has bound men through Christ to the Father, and made them members of that invisible Church whereof the visible is but the symbol and sacrament.

It is a belief that is shaped by the problem which it answers, in principle, as to the relation between the historical Christ and those who have never known Him according to the flesh but have been filled with His spirit—*animæ naturaliter christianæ*—who not having the Gospel have been a gospel unto themselves.

The history of this belief and of its gradual growth in definiteness illustrates well the selective power of the Christian spirit—of the *Lex Orandi* criterion. It passed through many phases of interpretation, according to the variations of theological or exegetical opinion, none of which secured a firm hold on the faith of the Church for lack of any definite prayer-value, until in the West it assumed its present form and significance which were felt by the spiritual instinct of Catholic Christianity to give a fuller and more harmonious development to the idea of the Incarnation.[1]

Turning now to the Resurrection, in what sense, we may ask, does St. Paul make the historical fact of Christ's bodily rising the central object of our faith? Is it simply as a miracle in the ordinary apologetical sense of the term? Is it that we are to pass from the evidence of the resurrection to a belief in Christ's claims to be the Son of God? Manifestly not; for of all the Gospel miracles this was, in one sense, the least evident, being witnessed only by the interested parties—by friends only, not by foes. In the classical passage on the subject,[2] it is clear that he is not proving Christ from the resurrection, but proving the resurrection

---

[1] Cf. *Étude historique sur la Descente du Christ aux enfers.* Par l'Abbé Turmel. *Annales de Phil. Chrétienne.* Fevrier, 1903.

[2] 1 Cor. xv.

from Christ. "If Christ be not risen then is our preaching vain, and your faith is also vain;" *i.e.* without the resurrection and glory the whole doctrine of the cross is incomplete; for it is an integral part of the conception of Christ. Even had He shown Himself to no one after His death, it would still be an article of faith. Life through death: victory through defeat: honour through dishonour: is the very substance of the Christian hope. As to the materialistic difficulties with which St. Paul deals: "How shall the dead rise? With what bodies shall they come?" they can hardly trouble us in these days when for many it is so much harder to believe in matter than in thought and spirit; when the whole tendency is to make the former a manifestation of the latter. The real difficulty for us lies rather in the seemingly undue weight attached to physical re-embodiment, and to the miraculous properties of the risen body; in an apparent materialisation of the conception of spiritual glory, altogether uncongenial to the whole trend of the gospel. That the dead in Christ shall rise, and rise to a more glorious life than that which they have laid down, is primarily a law of the moral and religious order, and has nothing to do with bodily death and life; but with a death unto sin and a new birth unto righteousness. Yet it is in close keeping with the whole economy of the Incarnation, which translated the invisible will-world into terms of the visible sense-world, and which is the dispensation of sacraments and symbols, of divine accommodations to human modes of thought and speech, that the visible life of Christ on earth should set forth in parable that invisible life which He leads in each Christianised soul; that as in its struggle heavenwards the soul after dying absolutely to self rises to a glorified life; so Christ after a life of labour and suffering culminating in death, should rise according to the body to a more glorious state of bodily life.

Again, it is the merit of Christianity to have recognised the unity of human nature as bodily and spiritual; to have saved in a higher synthesis whatever regulative truth was contained in that false dualism of which Plato is the classical exponent, and which issues practically in innumerable ascetic fallacies all based on an imaginary antagonism between what God has joined together as two elements in one nature. A merely ghostly resurrection would have given a strong impulse to this mischievous fashion of thought, as well as to a Docetan denial of the veritable (not merely phantasmal) manhood of Christ. It would have favoured the notion that man is by essence a spirit; and that his body is his prison. "A spirit hath not flesh and bones as ye see me to have."

Whatever the body be, it belongs to the integrity of human nature. Not only in it, but by it and with it, we live, and move, and are; and as it shares in our suffering so also in our glory. On this conception of the relation of body and soul rests the Christian view of temperance and purity, midway between those excesses of encratism on this side and antinomian licence on that—errors that play each into the hands of the other.

As for those who scorn the grossness of a bodily resurrection and take refuge in the idea that it was Christ's spirit that appeared to the apostles, let them reflect on the "grossness" implied in the notion of a spirit "appearing." If the appearance was objective, it was as gross as any other object of vision, and plainly cannot be identified with an immaterial spirit. And again, it may be asked, without much hope of a firm answer, how far are our own bodies and everything bodily that lies beyond them, the creatures of our thought? Is there not much grossness and materialism in speaking of matter as gross and as completely independent of and opposed to spirit?

XXV.

THE PRAYER-VALUE OF OTHER BELIEFS.

(3.)

MUCH that has been said of the Resurrection applies equally to the Ascension, which is its complement. But here the event viewed as a visible fact is more plainly an accommodation to human modes of thought, more obviously a bit of symbolism valuable not for its own sake but for the sake of its religious significance. The exaltation of humanity, through the death of self-sacrifice, to the closest union of quasi-equality with the divinity is the strict matter of faith, which is embodied and set forth symbolically in the phenomenal order by what occurred on Mount Olivet. We cannot suppose that "ascent" means more, here, than "descent" in the previous article; although here the idea seems to have been translated into appearances accommodated to the popular imagination of Heaven as the locality outside the concentric seven spheres whereof this earth was then thought to be the core. As to His enthronement at the Father's right hand, the Catholic Catechism is careful to explain the purely verbal, as opposed to phenomenal, nature of the symbolism: "I do not mean that God the Father has hands, for He is a spirit; but I mean that Christ as man is in the highest place in Heaven." Indeed, this phrase, "the highest place in Heaven," is burdened with the very difficulty it would explain unless we take it as expressing the purely spiritual relations of the will-world. "From thence," the Creed goes on, "He shall come to judge the quick and the dead," *i.e.* from the right hand of the Father, which has already been limited to a purely spiritual significance. If the *terminus a quo* of this second coming cannot be taken as a reality in the phenomenal world, how, it may be asked, can the advent itself be so taken? Yet the angel in shining garments — an appearance of an immaterial being — who consoles the upward-gazing Apostles, says "This same Jesus who is taken up into

Heaven shall *in like manner* come again even as ye have seen Him go up."

Is it possible to resist the impression that the revealed truth, the faith-matter of these articles, lies simply in the spiritual relations they signify, and that the words, or phenomena (subjective or objective) through which these religious truths are conveyed to us are of no other importance than as vehicles of these truths; even as sacramental symbols have no other importance save as means of grace? "It is the spirit that quickeneth; the flesh profiteth nothing."

The religious and the historical truth of Christ's Ascension are distinct from one another. The mere fact that His body was caught up into the clouds is of no religious value whatever, any more than the mere fact of His having walked on the water. The value of the latter fact is given to us in the exclamation it excited: "What manner of man is this?" *sc.* the supremacy of the divine and spiritual over the material order; the comprehension and absorption of the latter by the former. To narrate these wonders as wonders, and not as fraught with primary, and the internal aspect as of secondary, importance. It is antecedently likely that Christ who took the current Messianic ideas of His time, and purged them of their carnality, who gave Himself out as the *true* because the spiritual, Messiah (just as He was the *true* manna from Heaven) whose kingdom was not of this world, but a kingdom of Truth, should have adopted the current eschatology so closely bound up with the Messianic beliefs, and should have crowded a wealth of spiritual meaning into that very earthly framework. In neither case does He abruptly cast aside the old forms of traditional thought: He speaks as all around Him speak, but He means otherwise and more than they mean. The coarsest millennial theories; the most material figurings of heaven and hell, the most mercantile notions of reward and punishment — all receive at His hands a new and heavenly meaning and are made vehicles for the revelation of realities of a wholly different order. The real criterion of the religious truth of these beliefs in judgment, hell and heaven is: Do they bring the will into a right attitude Godwards? Do they make men love justice and hate iniquity? Without some such embodiment, the realities of the will-world would escape us altogether. In acting according to this presentment of the visible order we shall guide ourselves right in the invisible order, as it were, by a clue in a dark forest. If we let the clue slip, we may perish irrecoverably.

It will not be necessary to push this line of thought any further as regards the remaining articles of the Creed or other doctrinal beliefs of the Catholic religion; it only remains that we should see how far these principles are to be extended to the realm of morals as well as to that of faith.

XXVI.

ETHICAL BELIEFS.

As soon as men come to realise that God is necessarily a righteous God and that righteousness is another name for the will of God—for what God wills—the interests of religion and ethics are identified. Prior to this realisation the instinctive love of goodness is not explicitly understood as an instinctive desire of friendship and will-union with God. Indeed it is quite possible to will what God wills without the slightest suspicion that our will is therefore brought into harmony with His, and without any consequent sense of deepened personal affection towards Him. There may be a sort of emotional peace or pleasure resulting from the perfect satisfaction of our moral sense; or a happy consciousness of the merited approval of others—received or imagined: or a sense of the advantage resulting to society or to some cause to which we are devoted; or a lonely solace in the dry thought of duty done—of an eternal impersonal law fulfilled. All these satisfactions are distinct from that of religion.

A consideration of the development of the ethical sense before it is assumed and swallowed up by the religious sense will serve to illustrate, in another matter, that relation between sentiment and belief which is implied in the maxim: *Lex orandi, lex credendi.* For in the realm of morality the ethical creed is shaped under the influence and inspiration of the ethical sense; good-will—the desire to do, and therefore to know, what is right, what is due to others, what is due to reason, is the initiative and the selective principle of the whole progress of ethical thought. On the other hand, the theory of what is right reacts upon good-will and makes its further expansion possible; it is not merely its inoperative mental shadow, but rather an instrument fashioned by good-will for its own ends. For "good-will," the "desire to do right," is a general term for a sentiment that is by no means homogeneous and colourless, but which varies in character with every different conception of goodness and rightness; and as this conception is capable of indefinite growth in point of organic complexity and coherence, so too is the sentiment which corresponds to it and gives birth to it. When we say: "Good-will is everything," we do not mean that ethical judgment is nothing. A certain intensity of good-will may for a time be compatible with grossly erroneous ethical theories; but the character or quality of the sentiment corresponds exactly to that of the judgment—for the will is always specified or characterised by its object. "Good-will is everything" in the sense that a strong desire to know what is right will excuse sins of ignorance, and will lead to that fuller knowledge which will make a fuller goodness possible. Knowledge on the other hand is a liberating condition, but it is not an active motive of goodness. However vigorous and intense, the moral sentiment, like the religious, cannot germinate in the dark, but must remain undeveloped and poor in character until it find the means of building up a creed for itself, *i.e.* of feeling its way to a better knowledge of that realm of reality to which it has to adjust itself; of registering and fixing the results of its experience in some sort of ethical system; of determining its own true object and its own true character to something definite and organic from something shapeless and confused. Here too we have principles of variation and a principle of selection; the former, in the thousand moral, non-moral, or immoral sources of ethical beliefs, laws and customs, good or bad; the latter in good-will together with the already assured articles of the ethical creed. Here too in its measure avails the criterion " *Securus judicat orbis terrarum.*"

Ethical theories and beliefs that have experimentally been proved fruitful of moral vigour and advance, always, everywhere, in all cases, are thereby shown to be in harmony with Nature; to be truer than any merely reasoned counter-theory that has not stood that test. It is by this canon alone that numberless prohibitions, like that of suicide or of sundry sexual irregularities can be solidly justified ; and not by those sophistical reasonings of moralists which only imperil our faith in beliefs that seem to hang on so slender a syllogistic cobweb.

XXVII.

MORALITY AND RELIGION.

We have said that Charity or the love of God as revealed to us in Christ and in the Christlike, is the very substance of the life of religion.

When therefore St. Paul says that "love is the fulfilling of the law" and "love worketh no ill to his neighbour," he is showing how religion entails morality, as something distinct, but connected; he is not reducing all moral precepts to one, or bringing all particular laws under one general and abstract law—as, for example, all special kinds of justice, such as truth, honesty, equity, piety, might be enjoined in the one precept: Be just! Love may be a motive of morality, but it is not a virtue or moral habit in the ethical sense;[1] just as the

[1] Cf. St. Thomas, I-II. q. 62. a. 2. c. "Virtutes theologicæ specie distinguuntur a moralibus" *et alibi passim.*

passions pertain to morality only as the subject matter which it regulates. Morality is a certain rational and, in some sense artificial order introduced into our life, analogous to the order which logic (natural or acquired) introduces into our mind, or which the understanding introduces into our experience. But the life so regulated and set in order is an action or will-movement, continuous, many-sided, ceaselessly transforming itself into something newer and fuller. Whereas justice or any other sort of morality may be enjoined directly, love cannot be so enjoined. We can impede its growth and foster it; we can do the outward deeds and say the words of love; but over the thing itself we have no direct command. It is given to us, like the inspirations of genius; or it happens to us; and we can dispose ourselves to receive it and can co-operate with it when received; but it remains, in some sense, a grace, nor can we by taking thought add a foot to our own stature in the matter. The force of St. Paul's words is that we should not forget the end in the means, but should remember that "the law" is purely subservient to the love of our neighbour. An analogous error were that of a man who should consider logic a sufficient education for the mind and should despise knowledge which is the end to which logic is directed.

In the ethical categories of the Greeks, which have been adopted by the later Jewish and the Christian religions, Justice is almost synonymous with duty. Prudence, Fortitude, and Temperance, which look directly to the perfection of the individual in his practical judgment and the restraint of his passions, are ultimately sought in the interests of Justice; and if acts against Temperance or Fortitude are sinful, it is because indirectly they are against Justice, against what is due to God and to Society; because the individual, as part of the will-system and spiritual organism, does not belong to himself but to others. "You are not your own," says St. Paul, and: "Know ye not that your bodies are the members of Christ?"

Hence, we may identify morality with Justice, which is the giving to each one his due according to his place and function in the universal society, whereof God is the Head and Father. When God is not thus distinctly recognised, there is still place for the social sentiment of love, which becomes "charity" as soon as it is completed and coloured by the love of God and of all others in relation to Him.

Now, it is possible to have right views as to what is due to others, and to pay those dues with punctilious exactitude; and yet to be grievously lacking in love both towards God and man. And it is possible to have strongly developed social and religious affections, and yet through ignorance, or through frailty, to fail seriously in the knowledge and performance of one's duty. But whereas morality will not force a man to strive to be religious, religious and social love forces a man under pain of insincerity, to strive after morality, to strive to know what is due to others and to discharge the debt. Still, it is the will-attitude—the ethical effort—that counts before God; and not the ethical success. Thus morality is at once distinct from, and connected with religion. It is in the field of morality that charity is exercised; yet it is not the tillage but the exercise that is religiously important. But like science or philosophy it is only indirectly that ethics has to do with faith. Our ethical conceptions grow *pari passu* with our conceptions of society; they begin with seemingly arbitrary taboos, with mystical precepts and prohibitions, with puerile explanations of instinctive judgments and of accumulated experiences of utility; they are in all respects under the same law of endless progress as our scientific conceptions, and belong to the world of the understanding, not to that of faith. In what sense then can ethics belong to religious revelation?

No sane critic will contest that the sacred scriptures show us many grades of progressive morality all claiming in some sort to be of divine authority. How can we explain this except by recognising a certain selective power in the religious spirit which makes it instinctively choose that ethical doctrine which is more spiritual, and more congenial to itself—choose it, not as final and absolutely the best, but as preferable, as better than its alternative. This spirit may be initiative in some degree; it may inspire and suggest higher ethical conceptions than those current; but, as a rule, it will be rather as a selective principle that religion will shape the development of morality. If conceptions of duty are founded on conceptions of society, it cannot be denied that these latter are fundamentally religious conceptions in so far as the sentiments and will-attitudes which they seek to explain belong to the real world.

Hence, in every ethical system or doctrine, we must, as in the case of theological belief, distinguish between the principle of variation and the principle of selection, between the raw material, which is supplied by human industry and ingenuity, and the refinement which has been wrought thereon by religious inspiration—by the love of God and man seeking congenial expression in conduct. If religion interferes with this or that point of ethics, it is always in the interests of charity and not of ethics for its own sake. At times it may happen that religious ethical teaching is out of joint with some popular system of morality in certain particulars. In adhering to her position the Church but asserts the supremacy of love over the law, over that which is for the sake of love; nor may she change until it be made clear that the interests of charity will not suffer.

CONCLUSION.

We have spoken of the beliefs which make up the Christian creed as being in some sort sacramental; as signifying and conveying certain spiritual values under the forms of historical or philosophical truth; as belonging at once to the world of appearance and to the world of reality; as resembling a darkened glass through which some few feeble rays of the eternal sun fall upon our inward eye, and through which again we peer dimly into that unknown Beyond, and so guide our steps according to vague impressions of light and shade amid objects seen only in blurred outline. We have said that the need of harmony in our understanding, of coherence and unity in our mind, demands a continual adjustment between the historical and philosophical assertions of religion and the rest of our history and philosophy which we owe to the labour of the human understanding systematising and unifying the gathered experience of the race.

In periods of comparative intellectual stability, or even stagnation, such adjustment is effected easily, noiselessly and gradually; but in an age like the present when mental progress has changed the tranquil flow of a lazy river in its large and level channel for the rush of a swollen torrent leaping from cataract to cataract and bursting through every barrier, the span of a single life-time is not enough to see even an approach to a satisfactory reconciliation between the religious and the secular reading of the facts and connexions of the world as given in the understanding. More problems are offered for solution now in three decades than were formerly offered in three centuries, with the result that now a burden of difficulty is laid on the shoulders of a single generation that had then been divided over a whole series. As a consequence, the energies of the professed defenders and exponents of belief are more and more absorbed by controversial interests; and for the layman in theology, amid the clang of hammer and anvil, the grinding of blunted blades, the furbishing of ancient armour, the riveting of loosened links, all possibility of "peace in believing" seems to be well nigh departed. And yet this growing sense of insecurity is rooted in that confusion of mind which it has been the object of these pages to combat—the confusion between the intellectual and the religious values of the Christian creed; between the embodiment and the spirit embodied; between the outward sign and the inward power and significance. We forget that the issue is not directly between faith and knowledge, but between theology, which is one part of the field of knowledge, and the rest of the same field. Faith were imperilled if theology were an exact, necessary and adequate intellectual expression or embodiment of faith and if, as such, it came into demonstrable conflict with the indubitable data of history or science or philosophy.

To realise clearly the often comparatively loose relation between faith and its intellectual expression; to understand that a language derived from, and primarily adapted to, the visible world can never be adequate to the utterance of the invisible, is to have delivered one's soul from a whole brood of idle fears and fancies, and to have risen above the storm-level to a region of untroubled serenity: *Non in dialectica,* says Ambrose, "It is not through disputation that God has chosen to save His people;" it is not through theologians nor by theological methods, though these have their due place, but by the Holy Spirit, by the Spirit of Holiness working in His saints and servants, that He has promised to lead His Church into all truth. By that same Spirit He has from the beginning spoken through the mouth of His holy prophets, in sundry times and in divers manners,—to every time in its own language however rude and inadequate; and in these latter days He has spoken to us through His Son and through the Church of the Saints which is the mystical body of His Son. It is that Spirit of Holiness which from the first has suggested or selected now one belief and now another; weaving them together, purifying, correcting, refining, and so building up that complex organic body of doctrine which we possess in the Christian creed and which answers to that complex organic sentiment of divine love or charity of which it is the intellectual expression and justification. And it is this same Spirit of Holiness in ourselves that makes us responsive, each of us in our measure, to the truth when it is presented to us. If we hear the Shepherd's voice it is because we are already His sheep in some degree, and because the Christ that is within us recognises the Christ that is without us. Herein lies the religious or supernatural element of faith; the reasons we give to our mind are but after-justifications of an impulse that derives, not from reason, but from the sympathetic intuitions of the Spirit of Holiness.

It is however to the Church, to the mystical Body of Christ, to the Creed which incorporates the collective results of her spiritual experience, that we are to look for the norm or rule by which our own spiritual growth and religious beliefs are to be criticised. *Securus judicat orbis terrarum;* universality is the test of truth; only those beliefs which have been proved fruitful of eternal life everywhere, always, with all men —so far as they have been put to the test,

o

are demonstrably accordant to the ultimate realities of the supernatural order. Other beliefs may be useful for individuals or classes; for a certain period, for a certain type of character: and yet hurtful elsewhere and otherwise. Such have not the warrant of catholicity; the life which they foster and formulate is not the life of the *whole* Church, of the mystical Christ. And there are beliefs or devotions which originate in mere theological curiosity, or in pious fancifulness, or in morbid sentimentality, or are dictated by religious decadence and laxity; beliefs which are enervating or distracting or frivolous—in no sense exigencies of the spiritual life—and these, not having much root, are doomed sooner or later to wither away. From the continual and endless variations of belief and devotion which originate in one way or another, the Spirit of Holiness eventually selects and assimilates the good and useful, and throws away the worthless or mischievous, by the slow logic of spiritual life and experience. Hence the Church at large is the proper organ of this development of belief which results from the communising, comparison, and ordering of the religious experience of all those who have lived the Christian life in every age or country. Through her hierarchic organism her sundered parts are knit together and brought into dynamic connection; the manifold gifts and measures of love and light scattered abroad among the faithful are gathered as rays to a focus; their various spiritual energies are brought to bear upon one another, and thus there emerges a corporate life of love and belief which is more than, and distinct from, that of the several units who are partakers in it—for it is the life of the mystical Christ Himself.

When once we realise clearly that the Church is guided into all truth not by the precarious methods of theological dialectic, but by the Holy Ghost; that life and not logic is the ultimate criterion as to what beliefs and forms of belief are fit to survive; that eventually, and in the last resort, it is the Saints and their followers who discriminate between false and true, food and poison; that the doctrinal authority of the Pope and Bishops rests not on a special theological skill, but on an instinctive discrimination between holy doctrine and unholy, *i.e.* on the guidance of the Holy Ghost; then only shall we be delivered from the spiritually disastrous snare of confounding intellectual perplexities and entanglements with doubts against faith.

No theory of doctrinal development however true, however subtly flexible, can alleviate this ailment or supply us with a firm and simple principle of discrimination so long as it looks on that development as more or less principally an intellectual or theological movement, led and controlled by the mind in the interests of speculative truth; so long as it gives the lead to the *lex credendi*, —to the head rather than to the heart; so long as it makes sentiment wait upon idea; life and action upon knowledge; forgetting that we must live and act in order to discover the laws of life and action, and that we must keep Christ's commandments, if we would know His doctrine.

Development there is indeed, yet it is not one that is governed by dialectical laws but one that is dependent on and correlative with that development of the Spirit of Holiness in the Church at large of which it is but the mental expression, and whose metamorphoses it faithfully follows as a shadow does those of the body's contour, though, unlike the shadow, it co-operates with and reacts upon the movement which it follows.

And herein we part company with those who would bid us look underneath all varieties and transformations of religious expression in doctrine or ritual for one and the same simple homogeneous sentiment of God's Fatherhood and man's brotherhood in Christ, and find in this the unchangeable substance of pure religion and undefiled, albeit masked in a thousand strange and misleading disguises; this the kernel, the rest mere husk; this the quickening spirit, the rest unprofitable flesh.

For this would mean that, though variations of doctrinal and ritual expression may be governed and criticised by ascertainable laws, and may exhibit developments that are to be distinguished as false or as true to such laws, yet these are laws of thought, of language, or of symbolism, not of the life of religion; and that underneath these veils of varying texture, beauty and transparency it is ever the same changeless substance that is revealed, now more clearly, now more obscurely.

This were to deny that Charity, the Spirit of Divine Love, in the Church at large, as in the individual, is susceptive of true development—not merely of an increase of intensity, but of an endless unfolding and closer co-ordination of multiform possibilities latent in its first germ; it were also to ignore the chief function of religious beliefs in this work of development, which is that of both characterising and fixing each stage of the process, and so preparing the way for the next;—not merely that of setting new melodies to words ever the same. The music grows with, and answers to, the growth of the theme; as the Church prays, so she believes.

There is no doubt an element of truth that lends a charm to this false lure of primitive simplicity. In a grown man the direct and negative simplicity of a child is childishness; yet though he may not and cannot become a child, to become in some measure childlike, to make himself reflexly and positively what he was when Nature first gave him into his own hands, is the scope of all rightly directed moral endeavour. Normally, his first exercise of liberty is to shatter this simplicity to atoms; to go as far as may be from his infancy, to break up and explore the infinite possibilities of his nature; his subsequent task is to return homeward, to reconstruct freely, consciously, appreciatively what he has shattered; to consent understandingly to God's designs in his regard. This is the law of all moral and spiritual life.

The Church cannot be a child again; yet her progress is ever towards a more deeply intelligent and deliberate appropriation of that infused simplicity of aim, spirit and method that characterised her childhood. To this end it was needful that the first simple forms of thought and life in which her spirit was manifested should give place to an organic complexity in which the unity of that spirit was seemingly lost to be eventually found and recognised as persisting unbroken under all these diverse manifestations of its inexhaustible potentiality; that ever and again she should learn through solicitude about many things the sovereign value of the one thing needful, of that best part which shall not be taken from her.

"God's Fatherhood and man's brotherhood in Christ"—a simple conception, a simple sentiment; yes, but that growth of the conception given us in the Catholic creed springs from and furthers a corresponding growth in the richness and fulness of the sentiment:

Lex orandi, lex credendi.

www.ingramcontent.com/pod-product-compliance
Lightning Source LLC
Chambersburg PA
CBHW070732160426
43192CB00009B/1412